Austin —
Enjoy the

Doc

A Life in the Law

Advice for Young Lawyers

A Life in the Law

Advice for Young Lawyers

William S. Duffey, Jr.
Richard A. Schneider
EDITORS

AMERICAN BAR ASSOCIATION
Defending Liberty
Pursuing Justice

Cover design by ABA Publishing.

The materials contained herein represent the opinions and views of the authors and/ or the editors, and should not be construed to be the views or opinions of the law firms or companies with whom such persons are in partnership with, associated with, or employed by, nor of the American Bar Association unless adopted pursuant to the bylaws of the Association.

Nothing contained in this book is to be considered as the rendering of legal advice, either generally or in connection with any specific issue or case; nor do these materials purport to explain or interpret any specific bond or policy, or any provisions thereof, issued by any particular franchise company, or to render franchise or other professional advice. Readers are responsible for obtaining advice from their own lawyers or other professionals. This book and any forms and agreements herein are intended for educational and informational purposes only.

Printed in the United States of America.

13 12 11 10 09 5 4 3 2

Library of Congress Cataloging-in-Publication Data

A life in the law : advice for young lawyers / edited by William S. Duffey and Richard A. Schneider. — 1st ed.
    p. cm.
  ISBN-13: 978-1-60442-596-3
  ISBN-10: 1-60442-596-2
  1. Lawyers—United States—Biography. 2. Practice of law—United States. I. Duffey, William S. II. Schneider, Richard A.
  KF372.L54 2009
  340.092'2—dc22

                                                      2009030061

Discounts are available for books ordered in bulk. Special consideration is given to state bars, CLE programs, and other bar-related organizations. Inquire at Book Publishing, ABA Publishing, American Bar Association, 321 North Clark Street, Chicago, Illinois 60654-7598.

www.ababooks.org

Dedication

To our Mothers and Fathers who guided us in life.

Acknowledgments

All of us want to express our gratitude to the lawyers from across the country who contributed to this collection and who embraced the need to communicate to young lawyers the important values discussed between these covers. We appreciate the time they devoted to add their insight and wisdom to this collection. We also are grateful for the American Bar Association's willingness to publish this work and for its belief that what is said here will impact how we practice law, live life, and treat our colleagues. A special thanks to Erin Nevius, our editor. Erin was our superb, patient, thoughtful guide in this process. Thanks also to all of those who helped us, typed, proofread, and encouraged us to bring this book to life.

The Editors

Contents

Introduction

William Roper: So, now you give the Devil the benefit of law!

Sir Thomas More: Yes! What would you do? Cut a great road through the law to get after the Devil?

William Roper: Yes, I'd cut down every law in England to do that!

Sir Thomas More: Oh, And when the last law was down, and the Devil turned 'round on you, where would you hide, Roper, the laws all being flat? This country is planted thick with laws, from coast to coast, Man's laws, not God's! And if you cut them down, and you're just the man to do it, do you really think you could stand upright in the winds that would blow then? Yes, I'd give the Devil benefit of law, for my own safety's sake.

—Robert Bolt, *A Man for All Seasons*,
Act I (1954).

In his famous play, *A Man for All Seasons*, Robert Bolt tells the compelling story of Sir Thomas More—a lawyer who maintains his allegiance to the law even when it would be more expedient to cast it aside for his own self-interest and preservation. In his Socratic dialogue here with Roper, More illustrates the importance of extending the protections of the law even to those who would do mischief because doing so ultimately ensures that the law is available to protect all people. More, of course, is not simply a lawyer; he is also a father and a husband. His struggle to uphold the law affects his family, requiring him

to resist even his family's pleas that he abandon his principles to pre-
serve his comfortable lifestyle and avoid the penalty of death that he
eventually suffers. In the end, More refuses to be blown off course but
he is fully aware of the impact of his decisions on his family. It is telling about the man that his final letter, dispatched from his cell in the
Tower of London before his death, was to his daughter. It was a letter
of encouragement and comfort.

There are in our profession today strong winds that continue
to seek to blow lawyers off course—professionally, ethically, mor-
ally, relationally, and materially. Many of us are asking: What do
we expect from our lives as lawyers, and, more importantly, what
does the profession expect from us? What is important to us professionally? What are our obligations personally to our colleagues, our
friends, our families, and our children? Some lawyers find themselves
adrift and try to uncover the source of their gnawing dissatisfaction
and their lack of fulfillment. These are questions not unique to our
time, but perhaps they are now more acute and pervasive. The road
forward is not always clear, although we each can find heroes in the
law—men and women who have served well, lived ethically, and
found fulfillment, like Sir Thomas More and others after him.

This book was launched in the belief that there can be great
comfort in counseling with those who have gone before us—those
who can share their insights on a life lived well in the law. Experienced practitioners have long served as role models and mentors for
those entering our profession. The pace of modern practice, however, sometimes leaves less time for those relationships. This book
offers an opportunity to sit down with a diverse collection of lawyers
and share their perspectives on what it means to serve in our profession. Our contributors here write about the values of the profession,
our responsibility to our communities, and our duty of service to
clients, to the public and to each other. They also address trouble-
some issues about how hard lawyers are expected to work, and what
sacrifices we should and should not make.

In compiling this collection of essays, we sought to get inside the
calling to be a lawyer—why did we set out to be lawyers in the first
place? We explored tough issues like what it is like to represent a client whose life literally hangs on the willingness of a lawyer to help
without a fee. We hoped our contributors would comment not only
on what they thought was important in the law, but in life as well.
We searched out short, compelling reflections that we could read
over and over, one at a time or all at once. We hoped this collection

might serve for each of us and for each reader as an intimate personal mentor in pocket form.

In the end, we got all we bargained for and more. Judge Griffin Bell, Fifth Circuit Court of Appeals Judge appointed by President Kennedy and Attorney General under President Carter, offers his trademark, no-nonsense assessment of the values of the profession. He sets a high bar. Former Solicitor General Paul Clement, appointed by President George W. Bush, takes on the duty of candor. Chief Justice Leah Sears of the Supreme Court of Georgia, who was the youngest lawyer ever to sit on that Court at age 36 and the first woman and later the first African-American Chief Justice, takes the reader on an inside look at her astonishing life as a lawyer and mother, and her determination to find the right balance. And that is just the start. By the end of this collection, lawyers old, new, and lawyers-to-be have the sense that they have had intimate conversations with outstanding lawyers who open their hearts, tell their stories, and share the values that they live as practitioners.

There are roughly 1.1 million lawyers in the United States, and 150,000 law students. All of those women and men come to the law by different paths—some follow the example of family and friends, some come inspired by the deep conviction of a cause, some come to pursue wealth—the permutations are endless. We come through the gateways of law schools that train us to think as lawyers, that teach us the law, and that set our eyes on the high standards of living up to our weighty duties. In the end, our task is to use our talents as lawyers to serve—whether we do that as an advocate for a client, or as a judge, or as an elected or appointed official, or as a law professor, or in the countless other ways that lawyers serve the public at large. We share the journey with you, and hope to have this book with us at the ready should we ever feel that we are losing our way.

Editors
William S. Duffey, Jr
Richard A. Schneider

Co-Editors
Roy E. Barnes
Timothy W. Floyd

The Brass Ring
Chief Justice Leah Ward Sears

I WAS ALMOST AT the top of my game. Getting there had always been the driving force in my life. Until now.

It was during the Christmas season of 1983, and I was the lead associate assigned to a big corporate transaction. The deal was worth around $10 to $20 million, which was actually a medium-sized deal for the law firm where I worked. But for me, it was a big deal. A very big deal.

I had been at the firm more than five years, since I was 23. I have always been one of the youngest at whatever I did. I was 16 when I went to Cornell University and 36 when Governor Zell Miller appointed me to the Georgia Supreme Court. In fact, I am the youngest person ever to serve on the Court, and the first woman. I was always breaking through barriers, always reaching for that brass ring.

Back then, I had my sights set on becoming a partner at a large, prestigious law firm because to me becoming a partner meant you had attained a certain level of competence. To get there, I had to be the best. So I worked around the clock, arriving most mornings by 7:30 a.m., definitely not leaving before 6:30 p.m., working at least half a day on Saturdays, and dropping in at the office every Sunday. Even during the Christmas holidays, when there was a skeleton crew, I was there working.

I have never been a details woman. I am a "big picture" type of person. But at the time, details were the challenge before me as I worked on the deal. It was my job to do most of the paperwork, study all the documents, and make sure all the i's were dotted and the t's were crossed. The partner in charge was home for the holidays. I think he was annoyed that I kept calling him, asking him where various documents were. I was interrupting his time with his family.

At home, I was just starting mine. Six months earlier, after eight years of marriage to my former husband, Love, I had given birth to our first child, a son we named Addison. I was young and insecure about caring for my first baby. I was nervous. I was also anxious to return to work from maternity leave. To be honest, I was frustrated being cooped up in the house all day.

While I was working 24-7 on the deal, Love had a more normal 40-hour-a-week job with BellSouth Corporation—the kind of job that when your child gets sick, you can leave to take care of him. And one day, that's what happened.

About a week before Christmas, my husband, who was home for the holidays, took Addison to the pediatrician. I managed to slip away from work for a couple of hours to go with him. We knew something was not right. The baby would drink his formula, and it would go right through him. But the doctor told us nothing serious was wrong, and we should just keep an eye on him.

Several days later, Love called me at the office. "Leah," he said, his voice cracking, "Addison just doesn't look good." I told him to take Addison back to the pediatrician. This time, when the doctor examined the baby, she told Love to take him immediately to the hospital. Addison was dangerously dehydrated.

Again, my husband reached me at work. "Leah, they're putting him in the hospital."

I remember walking into Georgia Baptist Hospital, going down that long, white, cold hall looking for my child. A nurse met me in the hall. She was blonde and blue-eyed, wearing a uniform with happy, bright colors instead of the traditional plain white nurse's uniform. She knew I was headed for a rough time, so she steadied me.

When I walked into the room, I saw my baby, the size of a small bread box, in the middle of a big hospital bed. There was an intravenous needle stuck in the side of his head. His eyes were rolling back in their sockets. He was just lying there, his chubby brown legs and arms spread wide, his little fists balled up. I started screaming, "Addison, Addison, oh dear God, Addison!" The nurse held me.

Today, Addison is 26 years old. He is fine. In fact, he's more than fine. He lives in Manhattan and trades bonds and commodities on Wall Street. Of course, he remembers nothing about this episode. But I remember everything. It was a defining moment in my life. Addison got well. But I changed. In fact, I believe I am a judge today in part because one day my baby boy got sick.

I have always had mental conversations with myself. That day, as I stood by my child's bedside, here is what I asked myself: "This is your son. He needs you. Are you going to be there for him?"

I also said this: "You're born. You grow up. You spend your whole life laboring and sweating and struggling. At some point, age creeps up on you and before you know it, infirmities set in. Before your life is over, you need to have answered the question: What was it all for?"

My whole life had been driven by other people's notions of what success meant. And I always managed to grab that brass ring. But until that day, I had never really stopped to think about whether I really wanted what I had been striving for. Did I really want to be a partner in a large law firm? Was it a good fit? Or was it just another obstacle to overcome, another dragon to slay so I could say I had done it?

The day I saw Addison in the hospital, I had to face the fact that there was another person in my life I had to consider. I had a baby now, a child. I was responsible for a new life. So my career was going to have to fit into his life and my family's. I was going to be a mother and a wife first. The career would have to come second. I still wanted to be at the top of my game professionally. But I had to find a way to do that and be a good mother too. I needed to find balance. And I did not think I could do that at a law firm, not at that stage of my life.

Within a year, I had left my dear friends at the law firm to become a traffic court judge on the afternoon shift. It didn't pay as well as the firm did, and adjudicating red-light violations and jaywalking certainly wasn't nearly as intellectually stimulating. But I had more time to spend with my son, and that was good for the entire family. Of course, I had no idea this choice would put me on the path that would one day lead to my becoming the Chief Justice of the Supreme Court of Georgia.

Perhaps it sounds trite, but we all have to make choices, and sometimes that means making sacrifices. I have never made the kind of money I wanted to make. But at 54 years old I can say I have done the work I wanted to do. I have never had as much time for my children as I wanted to have. But I've had enough time to be a good mother to them. My point is that I have made sacrifices in all areas of my life, but nothing has been sacrificed totally. I am still committed to being the best professional I can be. But I have learned the value of balance. And for that I am very grateful. I have never been happier or more fulfilled.

One recent day, I was sitting in my chambers at the Judicial Building preparing to walk across the street to the Capitol. I was scheduled to speak at a luncheon of an old sorority of which I have been a member for many years. Just before I was to leave, my daughter Brennan, a student at Spelman College, called. She was born a few years after my son. She asked me to meet her for lunch so she could introduce me to her best friend's parents. They were in from out of town and wanted to meet me. She said she needed me to be there for her.

As Chief Justice, I am often expected to "bring greetings" to any number of events. But when these events conflict with time I need to spend with my family, I am no longer confused about what I should do. Being Chief Justice is a big responsibility and a great privilege, and I'm honored by it. But being my children's mother is an even bigger deal to me. No brass ring is worth more to me than my family.

I canceled my luncheon at the Capitol and left to be with my daughter.

Chief Justice Leah Ward Sears is the first woman and the youngest person ever to serve on the Georgia Supreme Court, where she was appointed in 1992. Chief Justice Sears served on the Georgia Supreme Court until July 1, 2009.

Chief Justice Sears was also the first black woman to serve as a Superior Court Judge when she was elected in 1988. Before ascending to the bench, Chief Justice Sears had a distinguished career in private practice at the Atlanta office of Alston & Bird. She was educated at Cornell University and Emory University School of Law, and she has a master's degree in the Appellate Judicial Process from the University of Virginia.

Our Responsibility to Justice

Sally Q. Yates

I HAVE SPENT THE MAJORITY of my professional life as a federal prosecutor. I have a great job. I get to do what I believe is right and just and fair every day in every case. It is an awesome responsibility and privilege. I have been particularly fortunate during my tenure as an Assistant United States Attorney to participate in a wide variety of challenging and meaningful cases. But as rewarding as I have found my experiences as a federal prosecutor, it was a civil case—my first trial—that was the most meaningful case I have ever had and that I expect that I will ever have.

I was a second-year associate at King & Spalding in Atlanta when Judge Griffin Bell assigned to me a pro bono case to represent Lovie Morrison in Barrow County, Georgia. Ms. Morrison's daughter had been represented by another King & Spalding partner years earlier through the Legal Aid Saturday Lawyer Program and she had kept his card. When her mother needed legal help, she called King & Spalding. Judge Bell had known my father and grandfather—both lawyers—and knew that they were from Barrow County, so he assigned the case to me.

Ms. Morrison was the first African-American landowner in Barrow County, Georgia. She had owned 92 acres of land since the 1930s, 6.2 acres of which had just been annexed by a real-estate developer building a subdivision. The problem was that Ms. Morrison, mistrustful of the white court system, had not timely recorded her deed, carrying it instead tucked inside her dress each day as she worked in the fields. By the time she did record it, a conflicting survey of property was on the books, which was now being used by the developer to lay claim to her land. In the 1930s in rural Georgia, Ms. Morrison had good reason not to trust the court system; in the late 1980s, that same system would be given another opportunity to earn her trust.

We filed an action to return the property to Ms. Morrison using a theory I had planned on forgetting after first-year property class—adverse possession. Ms. Morrison's family had made use of the land we were fighting over by washing their clothes in the stream that ran through it and cutting timber for firewood. As luck would have it, there was a witness to our client's use of the land, a woman by the name of Ruth Chancey, who was the matriarch of what was then known as the Dixie Mafia. Ms. Chancey's family knew of my client's use of the stream, because her family had used the stream at a different point to operate their still. We needed Ms. Chancey to testify, but she didn't have a warm feeling for the court system either; the last time she set foot in the courthouse her husband had been sent to the state penitentiary for life for killing a man and dumping him in a well. After many afternoons of iced tea on Ms. Chancey's porch, she agreed to cross the threshold of that courthouse again and testify.

The time came to try the case, and I needed help. Not only had I never tried a case, although I come from a family brimming with lawyers, I had never even seen a real trial. I went to the late Charlie Kirbo, who was then a senior partner in the firm and known to take young lawyers under his wing. To my delight and great relief, Mr. Kirbo agreed to help. From that moment on, Mr. Kirbo treated the Lovie Morrison case with the same determination and commitment that he would have the most significant matter for Coca-Cola. It would have never occurred to Mr. Kirbo to have done anything else. The same man who had been known as President Carter's "one-man kitchen cabinet," who had counseled national and international leaders, walked Ms. Morrison's land with me, strategized with me, and when the trial came, sat next to me and guided me. Mr. Kirbo demonstrated, not through any grandiose lectures, but through his own actions, a profound commitment to justice.

When the case was tried in this small town in Georgia, our client and her daughter were the only African-Americans in the courtroom. Opposing counsel had struck all the African-Americans from the jury pool. The defendant, his expert, and his lawyers were all personally known to many of the jurors. All logic would tell you that our client didn't have a chance of prevailing on an adverse-possession claim in this setting. But a remarkable thing happened in that jury room. That group of 12 jurors—who went to church with the defendant, used the defendant's lawyer as their own, and whose expert surveyor had surveyed most of their own properties—spoke the truth to resolve a dispute in a Southern court. I wish that I could claim that their verdict was because of something I had done, such as an inspirational closing or a blistering cross-examination. But the truth is, their verdict was in spite of my novice performance, not because of it. I wasn't so much an instrument of justice as a witness to it. Those 12 people were given an opportunity to do what was right, and they embraced it. Our client was not the only one who left that courthouse with a new belief in our system of justice; I believe those jurors left with a sense of pride at having taken their responsibility to heart and having done what was right. As lawyers, what a gift we have been given to be a part of that, and what a responsibility we have to safeguard it.

Ms. Morrison's case didn't make any headlines; it wasn't about a lot of money, and we didn't establish any new legal theories. But this experience demonstrated to me that justice is never more powerful than when it prevails in the simple righting of a wrong. In a way, representing Ms. Morrison spoiled me. I experienced how gratifying being a lawyer can be in a practice that reflects your own personal values—that gives you an opportunity to do what matters to you. I will always be grateful to Ms. Morrison for trusting me with something that meant so much to her, and to Mr. Kirbo, one of the all-time great legal heroes, for his incredible generosity.

Sally Quillian Yates is the First Assistant United States Attorney in the United States Attorney's Office for the Northern District of Georgia where she is charged with overseeing all criminal and civil cases in the office of approximately 80 attorneys. She served as the Acting United States Attorney from July through December 2004, and was the Chief of the Fraud and Public Corruption Section of the office from 1994 until 2002, where she supervised the prosecution of the office's white-collar matters. Ms. Yates has been with the United States Attorney's Office since 1989 and has handled a wide variety of complex public corruption and fraud matters. She was the lead prosecutor in the City of Atlanta corruption prosecutions and the prosecution of Centennial Olympic bomber Eric Rudolph. She is a fellow of the American College of Trial Lawyers. Ms. Yates graduated magna cum laude from the University of Georgia School of Law in 1986.

The Courage to Try Cases

Honorable William S. Duffey Jr.

As a federal judge, I am privileged to be assisted by very bright, engaging, and interesting law clerks with whom I develop strong personal relationships. But, as dictated by the great cycle of things, our time together concludes and they prepare to move on to other work. We always talk about what they will do next—will they practice by themselves, teach, join one of the big firms? Will they make deals or will they litigate?

Since our time together in our chambers focuses on courtroom work, we generally discuss whether they want a trial practice. If they are leaning toward litigating, we explore what that means and whether they are ready, not just to litigate, but to try the case if it is required. Do they have the courage, the resilience, the hard-work ethic, the preparation discipline, and the presentation skills to walk into the courtroom and present their case? These are questions all lawyers should ask themselves before embarking on a professional road that has the prospect of a trial at the end of it.

In my discussions with my clerks, I view it as my job to ask these hard questions. My clerks, after all, have to figure out life for themselves. My purpose is simply to give them some idea about how to approach their deliberations.

Before I arrived on the bench, I had the benefit of a long career in which I had spent a good bit of time in the courtroom. I had been a trial lawyer in the Air Force, a litigator at a big firm, Deputy Independent Counsel in the Whitewater Investigation, and a federal prosecutor as the United States Attorney in Atlanta. Before I embarked on that career, did I know all the ins and outs of life as a lawyer? Had I asked myself the hard questions of whether I was ready to do trial work? To tell the truth, I do not think I ever worked through all the issues, and I did learn a lot from being tossed into challenges and having to work through them. But along the way, I was lucky enough to see some very fine trial lawyers at work and I saw what it took to succeed and what questions should be asked by anyone considering the journey.

For many years, I was what we call in modern parlance a "litigator." I processed cases from the beginning to the end—the ending most often being a settlement or a decision on a dispositive motion. But the scope of a litigator's life also includes the ultimate prospect that the case will actually be tried. In truth, most matters are not tried, and there are some very fine lawyers who become partners or spend long careers in litigation without ever actually trying a case. Depositions and briefs become the most prevalent events in the modern litigator's life. This is in contrast to the history of my mentors, who report that they were forever in trial, nonstop, all gathered in some courthouse or another, not lost in a countrywide or worldwide web of depositions and discovery.

Lawyers who are making the decision for the first time to become litigators must always be mindful that a trial may be required to ultimately resolve a matter. The mere fact that trials may be rare does not mean you can prepare or proceed as if a trial will not be required in your case. You cannot be so frightened of or anxious about a trial that you settle on unfavorable terms. You must have the stuff and the stomach to walk into the courtroom to present your case. As my clerks know well, trial work is hard work, demanding long hours in the courtroom, and long hours getting ready to enter it. Trial work simply is harder than most lawyers, especially younger lawyers, can ever imagine.

I remember a criminal trial when I was a prosecutor in the Air Force. A senior enlisted member was charged with selling major quantities of narcotics to mechanics who worked on the flight line. The case centered on a particular transaction. Shortly before the trial started, the defense lawyer for the accused told us his client was going to rely on an alibi and they had an alibi witness. We clearly needed to speak with the witness. When we did, she told us that on a whim, she and the accused had decided one Saturday to visit Wakulla Springs, Florida. She had a strong recollection of their trip, including how long they visited at the springs, the weather that day, and the details of the drive. I was impressed with her memory, the details of her recollection, and how she communicated. In fact, I believed she was telling me the truth. The visit, she was sure, was on the same day of the major drug transaction on which we were relying in our prosecution.

As we neared the end of our interview, I decided simply to go back and get as many details about the visit as I could to further test her memory. When she elaborated on the details of their visit, she mentioned there was a wedding at the springs on the Saturday they visited. I asked her for the details. She described it as a beautiful affair outside under a trestle. The bride was an attractive young woman in her twenties who wore a long white gown with a veil. The bride's bouquet was made up of blue and white flowers.

We had only a couple of days before trial, so I called the Wakulla Springs office and confirmed that they had a wedding that Saturday, and, yes, it was outside. He suggested I call the florist who directed the wedding if I wanted further details. I did and asked him to check to see what he knew about a wedding on the Saturday in which I was interested. He confirmed that a wedding had occurred and he passed along the details about the wedding that he had recorded in his notebook. What he told me was interesting, and I asked if he was available to testify at trial. He said he was.

The defense called its alibi witness at trial, who testified about her visit to Wakulla Springs with the accused. After her direct examination, the defense counsel sat down with confidence—a bit smug, even. My cross was short. I asked the witness to describe the wedding she had seen. She did.

After the defense rested, I called one rebuttal witness: the flower shop owner. I asked him to describe the wedding he directed on the day the alibi witness visited. He remembered the occasion well. The bride was in her late thirties and, because she had been divorced, she elected to wear a short, off-white dress, not a long white wedding gown. He also testified that she insisted on fall colors for her flowers—orange, yellow, and brown—even though the florist told her these colors were not in keeping with a spring wedding. I then described the wedding the alibi witness had seen and, yes, he had directed it also. The wedding with the white dress and blue and white flowers was on the weekend following when the alibi witness thought she had been at the springs.

The alibi witness was honest but wrong about the date. The defense lawyer sat stone-faced, stunned during the testimony. There simply was nothing he could do to diminish the impact of the florist's

testimony. He had been used by his client. He knew it, the jury knew
it, and the accused knew it. The lawyer confided to me months later
that the trial had devastated him and his confidence, and in the following years he was less engaged in trial work.

What happened in that trial simply illustrates that courtroom
work is unpredictable, anxious, and very, very hard. When beaten
down, you have to pick yourself up and go on. There are instances
when I've seen lawyers unable to do that. The ones who do are
remarkable courtroom lawyers. People have to be wired a special
way to be successful, skilled trial advocates.

A trial is a dynamic process. The lawyers and court come to it
prepared for what they believe will happen. What they believe will
happen and what actually occurs often is vastly different. This is
because trials—civil and criminal—all center around human conduct and all evidence is presented by people with different motiva-
tions, biases, intellects, memories, agendas, gifts, and purposes. It
makes for the unpredictable, if not often the irrational. A trial lawyer
is obligated to try to predict the unpredictable and then manage it in
the trial process. Simply put, a trial never goes the way you expect.
What I have seen and experienced borders on the amazing, and it is
often—maybe always—nerve-wracking.

*   *   *

I am always curious when young lawyers come to discuss their careers
and tell me that they want to do litigation. I always ask: "How do
you know that?" The response is almost always the same—it's something they really "want to do," they think they would "be good at
it," or someone has told them they are persuasive speakers and ought
to be a litigator. Some tell me they really enjoyed moot court work
and believe they are gifted in trial advocacy. I cannot recall a single
lawyer who said he or she based the decision on watching trials or
helping in one.

I always ask aspiring litigators and trial lawyers whether they ever
have had long, serious discussions with someone who has tried cases.
Few have. I ask them for a candid assessment of what trials are all
about and what it takes to walk into a courtroom on the first trial
day knowing the unpredictability of what will happen in the days to
come. Few know.

The questions keep coming. How do you think you will do when
you walk into a courtroom with a client whose liberty or business is
at stake? Can you take on the sole responsibility to decide which wit-

nesses will testify, which arguments will be made, which objections will be asserted—and which will not? How do you know you will be good at this work? How do you know you are wired to excel in this environment? How do you know you will be fulfilled practicing in it? Do you know what is required in an environment that is dissimilar to anything you may have experienced in the past? What have you done to see what this is really like and how you will react to it?

These are basic and essential questions, the answers to which are required for anyone to decide whether they are suited for or want to engage in courtroom work. If you are not, you will not be able to fully represent your client, and your professional life threatens to be unpleasant and unfulfilling.

When I was the United States Attorney in Atlanta, we hired a new Assistant United States Attorney who had convinced me that she had what was needed to walk into a courtroom and represent the citizens of the United States in a criminal case. She worked in our office for several months before I began to hear rumors that she was thinking about leaving. A few weeks later she asked to meet with me to explain why she was returning to private practice. "As much as I thought I knew what I would be required to do and thought I was prepared and suited to prosecute cases," she said, "I just find I can't do this any longer. I simply cannot go on doing my work and prosecuting cases knowing that it ends up sending people to prison. It takes too much of a toll on me and I cannot continue in my position." Actually doing what she had before only imagined exposed the reality of the work and its human impact, and it finally showed her that she needed to follow a different path.

This story is in contrast to the experience of a law student I know. He decided to experience the courtroom environment by taking an internship in a public defender's office. While he knew this was not the best-paying summer job, I encouraged him to take it, because I knew it would expose him to real trial work. At the end of his summer, he was permitted to represent a client in an actual trial under the student practice rule in our state. He told me the case was not a strong one for his client, but he wanted to feel what it was like to represent a client in a real case. At the end of the trial, he called to tell me his client had been acquitted. I asked how he had pulled it off, and he described the cross-examination he conducted of a key witness and how that raised reasonable doubt about his client's guilt. The structure of his cross was thoughtful, but as in all trials, he told me of a couple of breaks he had not expected that allowed him to discredit the witness. As in all things, I believe it was the special combination of skill and a little luck. He eventually asked himself all the hard questions, and even though he had done well, he elected not to pursue a career as a litigator. He concluded that it was not a good fit for him—a wise, insightful, considered choice based on solid data learned early in his professional life.

In short, it is imperative for a lawyer to make a clear-eyed assessment from the start on whether he or she has the courage and determination to try cases. The first reason for such an assessment is professional. Our profession relies on the advocacy system—two competent attorneys each zealously representing their client's interests. If one of those lawyers fears the courtroom or even is apprehensive about it, or simply is not interested in that kind of work, it disrupts the advocacy system's balance of equally skilled and equally courageous counsel. When one lawyer in a case fears or is apprehensive about the prospect of a trial, the system becomes skewed.

I have been in cases where it was clear to me that my opposing counsel feared trial or was not ready. It became obvious and it opened opportunities to seek a result, short of trial, that favored my clients. Fear compels capitulation and, when it occurs, the advocacy balance is disrupted and results in resolutions that are not as just as they could be. There is something powerfully leveling in the litigation dynamics when the counselors on both sides have the fortitude to say: If we cannot resolve this ourselves, I am prepared to present my case to the jury. It levels the playing field every time.

The other reason to learn early on whether you have the desire to try a case is a practical one, especially for young lawyers in large practices. Most lawyers are able to do the day-to-day work of litigation knowing that someone above them is calling the final shots. Litigation makes you the final decision-maker—questions become acute and the practical implications of them real. Most lawyers in large firms do not try cases. Many today are elected partners in their firm never having had to represent a client in a trial proceeding. They often do not know whether they are up to this intense and difficult work until they are forced into it in their late thirties or forties. If they learn at that late stage that this is not the work for them, they find themselves stuck. At that age, it is harder to move to other practice fields, and unwillingness to go to trial could result in pressure to resolve cases prematurely and on unreasonable terms. To those who say this will not happen to them, I can simply say I have witnessed it more than once.

Our system of justice is the finest in the world. The trial of cases before juries is a fundamental premise of our democracy. That system works only when skilled lawyers, each representing a client zealously and professionally, have the courage and the wisdom to acknowledge that a trial may be the only forum to resolve a case. When these adversaries are evenly matched, evenly motivated, and evenly coura- geous, our system works and justice results. Aspiring young litigators must, at an early age, examine deeply and honestly whether they have the skill set, the temperament, and the courage to play their role in the system. If you have not yet done that evaluation, begin it now.

Judge William S. Duffey Jr. is a United States District Judge for the Northern District of Georgia. Prior to taking the bench, Judge Duffey served as the United States Attorney in Atlanta. He had previously served as Deputy Independent Counsel in charge of the Arkansas phase of the Whitewater Investigation. Before his current tour in public service, Judge Duffey had a distinguished career as a litigator in private practice. Judge Duffey graduated with honors from Drake University in 1973 and graduated cum laude in 1977 from the University of South Carolina School of Law.

Rediscovering Our Calling

Honorable Roy E. Barnes

NOVEMBER 5, 2002, BEGAN as every day had in the almost four years I had been governor. I woke up at 5:30 a.m. and went to my office in the Governor's Mansion to look at the reports of what had happened while I was asleep. An escaped prisoner, a mishap at one of our ports, and dozens of requests for some relief or another were typical of the overnight event reports I received. However, this day was different in an important respect. It was Election Day and I was up for reelection. The public polls had me leading by more than 10 points. Our internal polling showed a much closer race, and, as I looked out the window, I could see what a politician who depends on urban votes in north Georgia never wants to see. Rain—even worse, cold drizzle. And in southeast Georgia where rural white voters were still angry about my action in removing the Confederate battle emblem from Georgia's state flag, the skies were clear, with no rain in sight. It was, I knew, a recipe for Election Day disaster.

There is a ritual each time the governor comes and goes from the Executive Residence. At the entrance to the mansion, a state trooper stands at the guard house at attention and salutes as the governor passes. When it was raining, I always told my driver to tell the trooper not to come out. This morning, however, the state trooper ignored the request. There he stood at attention as I approached. I had my driver stop the car. The trooper looked me straight in the eye and crisply saluted. He knew. Defeat was imminent.

I have taught my children over the years that the true test of our mettle is not how we act in times of plenty and victory, but how we act in defeat. I decided that though defeat was difficult and bitter that Election Day, it was not going to define the rest of my life. Professionally, I have always been a lawyer first, and a public servant (or politician, if you prefer) second. In my personal life, family and faith are primary guiding principles. But it is being a lawyer that defines who I am. I am the only lawyer in my family, the first to graduate from college, much less law school. I always wanted to be a lawyer, because in my youth it was lawyers who changed the world. It was lawyers who desegregated the public schools, expanded the voting franchise, stood up to the powerful on behalf of the powerless. That was my ideal of a lawyer, and it was what I always wanted to be. So, it was the compelling call of my profession that I would return to the practice of law after serving as governor. But, as I returned to private practice, I took a detour for several months that changed my life and my view on how and why law should be practiced.

Steve Gottlieb has long served as the director of Atlanta Legal Aid. About a month before I was to leave office I put in a call to Steve. He was in New Zealand on a dream vacation that had been years in the planning. I told Steve's assistant I wanted to volunteer full-time at Atlanta Legal Aid for six months after I left office. She said she would pass the message on to Steve when she sent her daily e-mail to him. Steve thought somebody was pulling a joke on him and instructed his secretary: "Tell him to send a writing sample." She told Steve my request was sincere. When he finally accepted, I wanted to work with him—and Atlanta Legal Aid opened its arms to me.

To say the change in surroundings from the governor's office to those of Legal Aid was dramatic is an understatement. My office as governor was a huge space where 50 people could easily fit. My desk was the largest I have ever seen, with a hand-carved rendering of the Great Seal of Georgia on the front. The view outside my window had the vibrant city of Atlanta.

My office at Legal Aid, on the other hand, was small and sparse. Only one guest could sit at a time. If two showed up, one had to stand in the hall. My desk was barely four feet long. The computer wouldn't boot up. I shared a secretary with four lawyers.

The view outside my office was of a brick wall, but my view soon changed. A young woman who worked at Legal Aid had been born with only one hand. This disability never slowed her down or kept her from pursuing her dreams. She learned to make beautiful small stained-glass windows with only one hand. Soon after I arrived she made a window for me. On the day she gave it to me, and while she was there in my office, I hung it in my office window. The brick wall was now replaced by a piece of beautiful art made by a woman with a beautiful sense of self-determination. Suddenly my defeat in the governor's race was not as significant.

Atlanta Legal Aid is located in downtown Atlanta. We opened at 9 a.m. each morning. When I arrived in the morning I always was amazed at the number of people waiting in the cold outside the office. After a few weeks, I was equally amazed at the number of people who needed help. I was sad that we could help so few. Steve Krumm, a career legal services attorney and one of the backbones of the Legal Aid program, consoled me when he took me aside and said: "We work in a legal emergency room. We can only help the worst." In fact, only about 20 percent of those who qualify for legal services could be helped. Not because of lack of merit of their cause, but because Atlanta Legal Aid lacks funds and volunteers.

I can tell many stories about the clients I represented at Legal Aid, all of whom had compelling legal needs. Each of their stories affected me in a meaningful way. Let me share one of them here.

Alfreida Webb is an African-American woman who was raising two grandchildren. She had worked for the same employer for 25 years. On the way home one afternoon she was hit by an uninsured drunk driver. Her car was totally destroyed and she suffered severe injuries in the accident. Alfreida was now totally disabled. She had a little property damage coverage on her car, and, after she recovered enough from her injuries to be able to move about, she began to shop for a car to replace the one that was totaled in the accident. She was a prudent shopper who searched the Internet for a reputable used-car dealer. She found a dealer who promised a warranty with each sale and 0 percent financing on the car purchase. Alfreida went to the dealer's lot and told the salesman she needed a good reliable car to make her regular visits to the doctor and because she had grandchildren to take care of. She also told the salesman she only had $6,800 to spend—the amount her insurance company paid for the car she lost in the accident. The salesman brought a car around for her to see. He told Alfreida the car was reliable—a great car. "I have driven this car and it will not strand you," he said. The salesman told Alfreida the price of the car was $6,990, and the car lot would be glad to finance the $190 difference between the price of the car and the $6,800 Alfreida received from her insurance company. The salesman then added a $395 "document preparation fee," a warranty charge, and a $287 "title fee" charge (even though a title costs only $21) to the $190

principal. The total amount he persuaded Alfreida to finance was
$1,243.36. It was financed at a 29-percent annual percentage rate.

On the same day she bought the car, and only 45 miles after she
drove off the lot, the car broke down. When Alfreida couldn't get
it to start, she had the car towed back to the lot. The salesman was
nowhere to be found, and when she finally talked to the manager, he
told her the car was sold "as is" and it was now Alfreida's problem,
not his. "What about the warranty?" she asked. "It is good only after
a 30-day waiting period," was his reply. Alfreida did what most citizens would have done in the circumstances. She called the police and
told them she was the victim of a theft. The police came, and though
sympathetic, they told her this was a civil matter and she needed to
get a lawyer.

Alfreida didn't know what to do. In a few days she went to the
credit union at her former workplace and borrowed an amount sufficient to pay off the debt to the used-car dealer. She went to the
car lot to pay off the loan. She told them she wanted her car back.
The manager told Alfreida her car had been repossessed and resold to
satisfy the $1,243 debt. I later found out the car was sold netting the
dealer $10,000. The excess was never paid to Alfreida.

Alfreida was mad, as she was entitled to be. Unable to afford a
lawyer, she decided to represent herself. A resourceful woman, she
went to small claims court and filed suit. Representing herself against
the dealer, which was represented by a lawyer, the judge awarded
Alfreida $7,000. The dealer's lawyer, unhappy with this result for
his client, demanded a de novo trial by jury in the superior court—
a right he had under the law. Now faced with a jury trial, Alfreida
came to Legal Aid for help.

She told me her story and I told her "if they want a jury trial, we
will give them a jury trial." I amended the complaint to allege a count
for fraud, deceptive trade practices, and every other claim we could
assert to hold the dealer accountable. The case proceeded through
discovery—a story in and of itself. Finally, the case was ready for trial.
As we were getting ready to try the case, the FBI raided the dealer-
ship and arrested the owner for insurance fraud. Before we struck the
jury the lawyer representing the dealer approached me about a settlement. We settled for $18,000, cash up front.

As we walked out of the courthouse, I watched as Alfreida hob-
bled on her walking cane. I thought, what would have happened if
Alfreida had been forced to try her case before a jury without a lawyer? I wondered whether she would have been able to make it through

jury selection. What would have been worse, when Alfreida left the courthouse she likely would not only have lost her case, she would have lost faith in our judicial system. But, today she knows the system works. She hugged me and we parted. The story I believe she now tells to her family and friends is that justice is not just available for the powerful, but it also is available to the powerless. Alfreida and the memory of the others I met at Legal Aid remind me why I became a lawyer in the first place.

When my six months came to an end, all of the employees at Legal Aid hosted a little reception for me. I was sad and reluctant to leave. I told them, "My time at Legal Aid was the best experience of my life, and I have had some pretty good experiences." I still take on Legal Aid clients and each of the lawyers in our small five-person law firm contributes at least 10 percent of their time to pro bono work. You see, I want them to find their Alfreida.

Roy E. Barnes is the former Governor of Georgia (1998–2002), and one of the nation's preeminent trial lawyers. He was first elected to the Georgia State Senate at age 26 and served eight terms. For more than 30 years, he has tried both civil and criminal cases in Georgia and neighboring states. He has also been a devoted pro bono lawyer. In 2003, he received the John F. Kennedy Library Foundation Profiles in Courage Award.

The Five-Year Itch

Laura J. Hines

THE "SEVEN-YEAR ITCH," a pop-psychology phenomenon imagined in Billy Wilder's wonderfully antic 1955 film of the same name, contends that even happily married people will begin to question their spousal choices sometime shortly after celebrating their seventh wedding anniversary. Despite several comically unlikely fantasies involving a sexy new neighbor, Wilder's hero ultimately resists giving in to temptation and, with the so-called itch going successfully unscratched, everyone lives happily ever after. I write, however, in praise of the five-year itch (in my case) to reconsider one's initial legal career choice. The decision to commit professional infidelity, if you will, may be the best guarantor of your own personal happy ending.

The ability to change direction, to reinvent ourselves, to contemplate a wide range of possible opportunities, once came quite easily to most of us. As college students, we abandoned our majors, causes, and interests in favor of new ones almost instinctively, driven by forces ranging from a favorite professor, a provocative book, an intriguing class, or a simple quirk of youthful curiosity. There's a great song in the musical *Avenue Q*, called "I Wish I Could Go Back to College," where one character achingly recalls: "You sit in the quad, and think, 'Oh my God! I am totally gonna go far!'" The world was our oyster, our blank canvas, and it offered limitless possibilities.

The decision to attend law school itself likely sprung from this naturally curious state of mind. In my case, I was working in Washington, D.C., after college as a legislative assistant to a congressman from my home state. For me, the experience was a heady one—

walking the imposing halls of Congress every day, crossing paths with prominent politicians and celebrities, meeting with lobbyists twice my age. I quickly realized, however, that the parts of the job I found most attractive suggested that I might be better suited to the law than to politics. I enjoyed the work of researching, analyzing, and drafting memoranda on issues raised by proposed legislation, and I welcomed with nerdy enthusiasm the chance to help a constituent navigate a particularly byzantine federal bureaucracy or regulation. Political wrangling, trade-offs, and compromises held far less appeal to me than the policy debates, sometimes constitutional in nature, regarding what the law should be in a fair and just world.

Some of us approach law school with a specific direction and unwavering purpose in mind. One of my classmates, for example, regarded law school purely as the means by which to achieve his goal of becoming a patent attorney, and he cannily paid his way through school by drafting patents on the side. The rest of us, however, arrive with more general, often high-minded interests or alter our goals as our law school years unfold. My two summers spent working at large firms during law school served more clearly to eliminate possible specialties than to solidify my future career direction. I was even lucky enough to land a judicial clerkship after graduation. As legions of law clerks will attest, the judicial clerkship may well be the ideal first legal employment, albeit an intentionally short-lived one. It allows one to experience a virtual fourth year of legal education, gaining invaluable insights into the judicial system as well as particularized areas of law, showcasing some of the best and worst examples of legal advocacy and, inevitably, postponing the need to make any definitive decisions about one's legal future.

I spent an extraordinary year clerking in St. Paul, Minnesota, for the late Donald P. Lay, then Chief Judge of the United States Court of Appeals for the Eighth Circuit. Judge Lay stepped down as chief judge during my clerkship, taking a senior status that gave him the freedom to sit as a visiting judge on panels in the First and Second Circuits, and provided me the opportunity to glimpse the inner workings of three different courts of appeals. More important to this story, my clerkship afforded me the privilege of witnessing a man who not only approached his work with the wisdom and humility of a judicial Yoda, but who evinced on a daily basis an exceptional relish for the job he had held since the year after I was born. Precious few of us, of course, will be fortunate enough to serve as federal judges, but the boundless joy and commitment to his life's work that

Judge Lay embodied struck me as precisely the goal toward which we should all strive.

At my clerkship's end, I found myself succumbing to the siren song of the private law firm that had similarly lured most of my law school friends. I chose Arnold & Porter, a Washington, D.C., firm founded by New Deal reformers with an impressive record of pro bono service and a wide range of practice areas I hoped to have the latitude to explore. After several months of a transactional practice, I volunteered for a pro bono project to draft an appellate amicus curiae brief. My work with one of the senior attorneys on this project led me to join the litigation group tasked with defending a series of high-profile class action lawsuits.

I absolutely thrived in my work on these cutting-edge cases brought by an array of high-powered and innovative plaintiffs' attorneys. Class-action litigation in both state and federal courts had reached a virtual fever pitch by the mid-1990s, with ever-expanding interpretations of what constituted a certifiable class. The stakes for our client, for the entire industry that conducted a joint defense in these cases, were enormous. One case in particular, a nationwide federal class action filed in New Orleans, consumed the majority of my time for almost two years, with all-night brief-writing sessions, primers on statistical models, multistate comparative tort law surveys, and strategy meetings.

So I found myself happily engaged in a richly challenging set of legal issues, working with two senior attorneys who exemplified my ideals of integrity and intellectual rigor, and who possessed unparalleled legal writing and advocacy instincts. Moreover, I was in the process of becoming enmeshed in the fabric of the firm, serving on committees and co-chairing the summer associate program. Why then, five years out of law school, did I experience an ultimately compelling itch to walk away from this attractive and promising career? In short, because I became convinced that my potential as a law professor held even greater promise for my long-term happiness.

My exposure to the complex world of mass tort class actions had made me crave the luxury of reflecting on its most intriguing facets on my own initiative, and not at the behest of any particular client. I was drawn to an occupation that offered me the complete freedom to think and write about legal issues from whatever policy, historical, empirical, or theoretical perspective I chose to pursue. As self-indulgent as that may sound, I hasten to point out that academic hours are not shorter, and the work is not easier than that of a law firm attorney. But the hours are almost entirely yours to define, and I cherish the fact that as often as I stay up until 3 a.m. typing on my laptop in my bathrobe like an intensely dedicated blogger, I am also free to spend the occasional sunny afternoon at the park with my three-year old. I left practice before the advent of mandatory Blackberry accessibility, but I well remember plans dashed at the last moment because of an e-mail or phone call citing an urgent client matter. My weekends and vacations may still include unexpected work commitments, but at least I have no one to blame for that state of affairs except myself.

In addition to the implacable urge for intellectual (and individual) autonomy, my decision to switch careers also was inspired by the rewarding examples of public service that I observed during my brief legislative experience. As much as it may sound like pie-eyed idealism, I wholeheartedly believe in the vital function that well-trained lawyers serve in every aspect of our political, commercial, social, and judicial systems, and I take tremendous pride in the part I play in the education of those lawyers at a public law school.

Ultimately, my soul searching led me to reflect on the lawyers I had seen pursue their fields of law with the same unbridled love of the game you can see on Dara Torres's face when she touches the pool wall to win an Olympic medal. I thought about Judge Lay, and about Barney Frank, whose passion and awe-inspiring oratory I vividly recalled from my Capitol Hill days. I thought about attorneys like Claire Reade, Jim Sandman, and Mel Spaeth, who still perceive each legal challenge with the gleeful eyes of kids in a candy store. Most of all, I thought about law professors like James J. White, Rebecca Eisenberg, Yale Kamisar, and my own father, Bill Hines, who still truly revels in his profession after nearly 50 years as a scholar. I concluded that becoming a law professor offered me the best chance at achieving that degree of career satisfaction, waking up each day not just well-contented in my work but delighting in it. An ambitious goal, admittedly, but one I can honestly report I have thus far accomplished at the University of Kansas.

Now my itch came at the five-year mark, but some of you will feel that niggling sense (if not grim certainty) that your happiness lies in another direction within a few years or even months after landing your first law job. Whenever that moment arises, I urge you to pay close attention to your instincts, just as you did when they steered you to law school in the first place. And beware of the strong inertial forces potentially arrayed against any such movement. You may feel indebted to the employer that gave you your first job, fear the dislocation of uprooting yourself or your family, or simply balk at any course that rocks your comfortable and familiar boat. Leaving private practice for seemingly greener pastures often entails a pay cut, and reinventing oneself can mean rigorous new hurdles to overcome: my law school roommate's job changes necessitated sitting for three state bar exams in ten years.

Some of my happiest and most successful friends, however, walked away from the lucrative world of corporate lawyering to become government attorneys at places like the Department of Justice and the Food & Drug Administration, found their true calling in the nonprofit sector, or left the safety of practice altogether to pursue careers in screenwriting, venture capitalism, or politics. My own move into academia required me to endure both a substantial salary reduction and a personally difficult move from a city and friends I adored to a college town in Kansas where I knew no one. Such disincentives and risks can certainly tamp down the temptation you might experience to choose a new and better path, but none should actually deter you when the stakes are so high.

More pragmatically, I advise you to keep your eyes on the lookout for opportunities that strike you as intriguing, keep your resume updated, and keep your connections with friends and colleagues intact. In my case, I stayed in touch with my most loyal supporter from law school, Kent Syverud, who was my Civil Procedure professor at Michigan before he embarked on stellar deanships at Vanderbilt and Washington University in St. Louis. Kent had fostered the idea of an academic life for me while I was still a student, and he responded with welcome and enthusiastic alacrity when I sought out his guidance on how to realize that goal. Updating your resume, while seemingly generic advice, forces reflection on your career arc and encourages frequent self-evaluation. It also eliminates the need for a massive curriculum vitae overhaul that could represent a daunting obstacle to applying for a new job.

For those among you who indeed feel an itch but cautiously resist acting on it, your risk aversion could well prove to be a healthy survival impulse. But I would urge you to consider opportunities that may allow you to have your cake and eat it too: take on a pro bono client; sign up to teach as an adjunct at a nearby law school; tackle a leadership role as a volunteer in your local community. You might also explore the possibility of taking a brief leave from your current job in order to check out another. Many firms will accommodate valued lawyers who wish to rejoin their ranks by leaving the window open for a possible return if the new opportunity does not pan out. One law school friend left her firm to spend time with her young children, returning when they reached school age. Such fluidity often works to a firm's advantage, as another friend found when he was warmly welcomed back from his stint as an Assistant United States Attorney with all the criminal trial experience that post entailed.

As for those of you who never perceive an itch to scratch or even a twinge of discontent, I applaud the prescience and dash of luck that led you straight out of law school into your dream jobs. Indeed, a handful of my own law school and law firm friends continue to thrive and flourish in private practice. But I still recommend the occasional exercise of self-assessment, perhaps every five years, to ensure that your contentment has not morphed into mere complacency.

Finally, if the itch you've scratched doesn't lead you to the idyllic future you thought it would, do not panic. Your happy ending is still out there. Remember, we lawyers are hard-wired with the ability to attack every challenge with well-reasoned analysis and the mental agility to identify winning alternatives. That skill set gives you the option to write and re-write the many chapters of your professional career as often as the itch may strike you.

Laura J. Hines is a Professor of Law at the University of Kansas School of Law. She earned her A.B. in American History at Brown University, and her J.D. at the University of Michigan Law School, where she served as a Note Editor on the Michigan Law Review. *After serving as a law clerk to the Honorable Donald P. Lay, Chief Judge of the United States Court of Appeals for the Eighth Circuit, she joined Arnold & Porter in Washington, D.C., where her practice primarily involved mass tort class action litigation. Professor Hines's scholarship has focused on the intersection of civil procedure and tort law, with a focus on aggregate litigation and punitive damages.*

How I Became a Lawyer
David E. Kendall

I WAS GOING TO BE A DOCTOR. In the small Indiana farming community where I grew up, doctors were revered. Lawyers . . . were not. This ambition, when stated, earned me warm—if cheap—regard from adults.

My ambition began to change when, as a college student, I worked for the Mississippi Summer Project, trying to register black voters in that state during the summer of 1964. It was in some ways a scary time. My roommate for the MSP summer training session in Oxford, Ohio, Andy Goodman, was one of the three civil rights workers murdered in Neshoba County, Mississippi, a few days after they returned to the state from the training session.

I felt deeply committed to the goals of racial equality and nondiscriminatory voter registration but increasingly uncomfortable with the heated rhetoric and seemingly endless staff meetings of "movement life" that summer in Holly Springs. But at the same time, I was attracted to the civil rights lawyers who represented us voter registration workers when we got arrested or jailed for specious alleged infractions.

Our lawyers, it turned out, had a powerful weapon in their hands, and I began to regard the law in a new way. Our lawyers didn't speechify; they marshaled facts, filed affidavits and pleadings, appeared in court and argued skillfully—they got themselves listened to and, it seemed, even occasionally feared by the "white power structure" that seemed to be so successfully harassing us would-be voter registerers.

These lawyers were cool (in at least two senses), fearless, and they got things done. They represented us aggressively and unapologetically. They knew the rules of a mysterious and tricky game, and they played that game skillfully against ill-intentioned opponents who often seemed less knowledgeable about the law. Our lawyers sometimes (though not always) marshaled in legal parlance for a public and hostile audience the fire and rhetoric we civilians used in our own speeches, writings, and meetings.

My relations with my defense counsel were not always happy for me, but they were instructive. Henry Aronson (I think it was) told me on one of my arrests that I had been so incredibly stupid to be stopped for driving my Volkswagen with Mississippi plates but without a Mississippi inspection sticker that I had no defense and he was going to plead guilty. And he did. On another occasion, Faith Seidenberg was representing me after I had been jailed three days for "investigation." Finally brought before a magistrate, I was handed the arrest warrant, I read it, and then I announced loudly, with what I thought was witty bravado, "There's something wrong here—this warrant says 'Take the body of John Doe'—I'm not John Doe!" Pandemonium erupted in the courtroom. Faith whispered in my ear, as she smiled winningly at the glowering magistrate, "I'm your lawyer. When I want you to talk, you'll talk. Unless I tell you to talk, keep your mouth shut." I nodded meekly, and she got the warrant dismissed and me out of jail.

I returned to college and, although I applied to and was accepted at various medical schools, I finally decided to go to law school, largely as a result of my Mississippi experiences. To my parents' great credit, I never heard a syllable of lament from them, although I am certain I know what they secretly felt about my choice. After graduate school, law school, a clerkship, and the Army, I spent the first five years of my professional life as a staff lawyer for the NAACP Legal Defense & Educational Fund, Inc., doing civil rights litigation, but uncomfortably aware that I was neither as skillful—nor as cool—as the lawyers who had represented me in 1964 Mississippi.

David Kendall studied at Oxford as a Rhodes Scholar and graduated from Yale Law School. He clerked for Justice Byron R. White. He served for five years as associate counsel at the NAACP Legal Defense & Educational Fund, Inc. Mr. Kendall currently is a partner at Williams & Connolly LLP. He represented President and Mrs. Clinton at the Whitewater Independent Counsel Investigation and related actions and currently represents them in miscellaneous legal matters.

The Balancing Influence of Interests Outside the Law

Richard A. Schneider

IN 1829, JUSTICE JOSEPH STORY famously observed that "[the law] is a jealous mistress and requires a long and constant courtship. It is not to be won by trifling favors, but by lavish homage." I confess that for at least the first decade of my life as a practicing lawyer, I swore silent allegiance to this old chestnut and did virtually nothing other than constant courtship and lavish homage. Eventually, I began to observe that the very best lawyers had lives and interests in addition to the law. Those outside interests made those lawyers better lawyers, more interesting to clients, more attuned to nuance, and definitely more fun to be around. Looking back from the perspective of 25-plus years, it occurs to me now that giving in to life is what has made my journey in the legal profession rich and rewarding.

Before pursuing a legal career, my sights were set on literature—novels and poems primarily, with an occasional dalliance in the field of songwriting, where literature and music meet. In my last year of college, however, I took a course in Constitutional Law, and read Anthony Lewis's book, *Gideon's Trumpet*. That book tells the story of *Gideon v. Wainwright*, the landmark Supreme Court decision that established the constitutional right to counsel in a criminal case involving a risk of imprisonment. I became fascinated by the law, and it was not long before I switched gears entirely and reset my sights from the arts to the law. I gave my heart fully to the new enterprise, becoming the most earnest of law students, followed by a completely absorbing adventure as a young associate and then a partner at a large law firm. I was consumed by my own drive to put forth my very best work product, to conduct my very best examination, to make the most compelling argument possible, which required an endlessly deep dive into the law and the facts. I learned what Judge Story observed. The law was relentless and exhausting.

Not realizing that I needed an outlet and a place to reenergize, an outlet was thrust upon me in a bit of musical serendipity. In a casual exchange in 1988 and for reasons that I can no longer recall, one of my law partners advised me that he kept safe and sound in his attic a 1968 Martin D-28 guitar given to him by his father for a long ago birthday—a guitar that had seldom been played. Intrigued, I asked if I might take a look at that guitar and perhaps borrow it for a bit. A short while later, we ransomed that guitar from the attic and I took it home. Eight years later, I still had the guitar and I had ridden its magic powers back into the world of music and literature. I rediscovered my love of songs and songwriting. And after long days in the vineyards of the law, I found myself with a six-string respite and relief each evening.

Finding my own outlet opened my eyes to my colleagues. Driven and obsessed by the law, I had not focused on the swirling world of interests that made up the lives of my friends and fellow lawyers. I discovered lawyers deeply involved in politics, running campaigns, serving on think tanks, going off to conventions. Here were lawyers with a passion for the symphony, for photography, for museums of modern art, for the theater, for representation of the indigent, for supporting charities devoted to fighting autism, cancer, diabetes, heart disease, and other conditions. There were lawyers as well devoted to lawyer-related groups like the American College of Trial Lawyers or the American Bar Association or the State Bar. Some devoted themselves to becoming accomplished at golf or tennis or mountain-biking. When I opened my eyes to all of this, it became clear that being a good lawyer—remaining energized and alert—required a balanced life and outside interests.

For me, I followed the sound of that attic-bound guitar back to the roots of myself. I began writing songs in earnest, and I eventually recorded a CD of my songs in 2003, with the high-sounding title of *Choices and Chances*. In 2006, I released a collection of my songs performed by some stellar musicians called *Second Chances*, produced by Jeff Jacobs, who played with Foreigner for 20 years and Ben Wisch. (Some of my more cynical partners have suggested that I name my next CD *Fat Chance* or *No Chance*—but I have rejected both titles.)

My musical sidelight reinvigorated my interest in poetry, and I began writing poems again. Lawyers and poetry are old and strange bedfellows, of course. Clarence Darrow said that "[i]nside every law-yer is the wreck of a poet"—although the great lawyer-poets, includ-ing Archibald MacLeish, Edgar Lee Masters, and Wallace Stevens, would disagree. As I was writing this short essay on outside interests, I recalled a poem that I had written about a talented lawyer who was quite a clarinet player—my beloved law partner, Bill Hendricks, who died of melanoma at age 56. Bill had a long and distinguished career as a prosecutor at the Department of Justice before going into private practice with us. Bill was one of the best lawyers I have ever had the privilege to work with—and he played the clarinet so skillfully that he was a regular performer with the symphony in Washington! Even before he died, I knew that Bill Hendricks was a fantastic lawyer because he was a complete person.[1]

---

[1] In Memory of William C. Hendricks, III

I see death holds you
like a handful of fireflies
held by a child some dark summer evening—
the way the blonde light leaps out
fluorescent
soft as powder
streaming between those helpless fingers
radiating across the silent night.
There are not any hands
that could ever contain that light.

Your hands too I well remember
orchestrating your phrases
keeping cadence in your renaissance minutes,
bringing the point up, down, gently, now louder—
pausing only to pull each cuff back into place
all the while leading with those hands
that could cradle a clarinet
or a jury
or an elegant cigar
with sheer delight and equal grace.

When they ask me
whose light is shining in the distant darkness,
I will tell them
it is the midnight oil of a lawyer's lawyer.
It is your luminous mark of day
upon the face of night.
There are not any hands
that could ever contain that light.

Being a lawyer is a privilege and a challenging assignment. The highest calling of every lawyer is to be first a good lawyer—and to spend time developing tremendous affection for the law, the facts, and the small details that it takes to succeed and serve our clients well. Returning refreshed to that assignment each day flows in part from the thrill of the challenge and the reality of a deadline. But it also flows from living a complete life in which you are energized both by your practice and your pursuits. The law is everything—but it is your little something extra that will end up rounding out your life, giving you a place to unwind, and sharpening your legal skills in the balance.

Richard A. "Doc" Schneider is a Senior Partner at King & Spalding in Atlanta where he specializes in the defense of tort and business litigation class actions. He is a Trustee of Mercer University, as well as a Trustee of the United States Supreme Court Historical Society. He attended the United States Naval Academy (1975–77), and graduated from Auburn University with High Honors in 1978 and Mercer University School of Law, where he graduated summa cum laude in 1981.

CHAPTER 8

The Values of Our Profession
Honorable Griffin B. Bell

I AM A LAWYER. Because I am a lawyer, I am obligated to follow ethical and professional standards, some of which are peculiar to lawyers. What are these standards and how are they made known to lawyers?

Every American is exposed to the fundamental values of truth and honesty as a child at the hands of parents and teachers. These values apply to every citizen, including lawyers. However, lawyers are further trained on ethical and professional principles in law school and from mentors, including jurists. Much is learned from history and from examples in court decisions revolving around actual facts. Other values are established by practices and customs and in exchanges between and among lawyers.

A good beginning is to be found in the rules of courts, state bar rules, and the ethical codes formulated by other professional associations.

Another good beginning is found in Sandberg's *Life of Lincoln*, in the last chapter entitled, "A Tree Is Best Measured When It Is Down," which contains many of the tributes paid to President Lincoln after his death. Tolstoy is quoted as saying that Lincoln was greater than Alexander the Great or George Washington because all of his acts embraced the principles of truth, justice, humanity, and piety. These same principles apply to us all in some degree, but they are bedrocks for lawyers. And it is important to remember that Lincoln was a practicing lawyer before his presidency.

We can also find examples of ethical principles when considering the obligation of lawyers to clients. One of them is that a lawyer owes undivided allegiance to the client. Another is that the lawyer must use the utmost application of his or her skill and industry to protect and enforce legitimate interests of the client. In doing so, the lawyer cannot be influenced by considerations of self-interest.

There are other general principles that guide the conduct of the responsible lawyer. One is to consider the public interest in the matter at hand and another is the spirit of magnanimity in victory. Still another is the obligation to finish a representation once undertaken, unless relieved for good cause by the client or the court. Finally, a lawyer has the obligation to remember the work ethic and that there can be no flagging or slacking once a representation is undertaken.

Public prosecutors should employ only neutral principles in making prosecutorial decisions and always without fear or favor. A prosecutor represents the sovereign and has the duty to see that justice is done, as between the sovereign and the defendant. Given the harm of an indictment without a subsequent conviction, there should not be an indictment absent a probability of conviction.

And it is the professional obligation of every lawyer to render public-interest legal service personally and by supporting organizations that provide legal services to persons of inadequate means.

What ethical standards apply in the relationship with opposing counsel? Here a lawyer owes the duty of courtesy, candor in pursuit of truth, cooperation in all respects not inconsistent with the client's interests, and strict observance of all mutual understandings.

A lawyer's word is his or her bond. I learned that as a young lawyer in Savannah some 60 years ago. Then, I was told by the senior lawyer in the firm that I was in at that time, "You can take the word of any lawyer in Savannah except one." At that time, unlike our time, agreements or understandings were seldom put in writing. Such understandings were more of a mark of the professionalism of the bar than an ethical standard and could be grouped with the professional obligations of courtesy, civility, mutual respect, good manners, and dignity at all times.

What is the ethical duty of the lawyer to the court? The lawyer owes the court respect, diligence, candor, punctuality, and protection against unjust criticism. There is likewise a professional obligation to maintain the dignity and independence of the courts. The lawyer must also maintain the highest principles of professional rectitude irrespective of the desires of clients or others. One obligation that is at the heart of professional and ethical responsibilities is sometimes not understood by the public, and that is the standard that the lawyer is not to be deterred in the representation of a client by public unpopularity or judicial disfavor.

And it goes without saying that during a representation no decent lawyer would be involved in withholding documents or other evidence when required to produce, failing in the obligation of candor, or cutting corners in any part of litigation, such as misstating an authority. Such conduct is a form of dishonesty.

Professionalism requires a lawyer to have a heightened sense of the public interest to the extent it does not interfere with a client's interest. The public-interest motivation should be to act for the betterment of society and the best interests of our state and nation. It would be a great disservice to separate the skilled lawyers of our state and nation from activities that further the public interest. Lawyers should be at the forefront in counseling clients with the public interest in mind.

This means that as lawyers, we should take into consideration the broader interests in deciding the proper resolution of disputes. An example I have experienced more than once would be having the employees and creditors of a corporation in mind when making litigation decisions, such as pursuing or continuing litigation that might possibly result in at best a Pyrrhic victory that might ultimately disserve the interest of the company as well as its people.

This obligation can sometimes be seen even in victory. As in medicine, treatment should render the least harm. Why create greater harm than what is needed in the victory?

There is no better example of magnanimity in victory than in the terms of the surrender of General Lee and his army to General Grant in the American Civil War. President Lincoln, General Grant, and General Sherman met at the Union Army staging area on the James River at City Point, Virginia, shortly before the surrender and when the victory was assured, to decide what to do with the Southern Armies. President Lincoln had instructed General Grant, "Let them off light. I want them back in the Union." And that is what happened. Lee was surprised at the magnanimity of the terms, and the same terms were later given to General Johnston by General Sherman.

Lawyers need to be well versed in history and to follow its teaching in bringing wisdom and good judgment to their decisions. Indeed, the highest service of the lawyer is in providing good judgment to clients.

Dealing with clients or with other lawyers in cases involving multiple lawyers is not always easy. First, take care when representing a client who thinks that he or she knows more law and legal procedure

than you. The lawyer must avoid being a mere mouthpiece and should
resign under most such circumstances. The same is the case where a
client or co-counsel suggests violating a rule of court or a professional
duty, such as not producing documents or misleading the opponent or
the court.

Each lawyer is the keeper of his or her ethics and professionalism,
regardless of what others, even clients, employers, or co-counsel, may
believe or direct. I have so stated to all lawyers with whom I have
been associated over the years. There are many settings in which ethical questions may arise. A few examples might be helpful.

Having been asked to assist a client already represented by another
firm in a government investigation and a possible indictment, I was
in a joint meeting with the client and the co-counsel when there was
a suggestion of some legal action being taken that I considered to be
unethical. I gathered my papers, closed my briefcase, and directed
one of my young partners who was with me to do likewise. I then
announced that we were leaving the case because we did not practice
law in that manner. The general counsel of the client was in the meeting and asked me to wait a few minutes while he conferred with the
chief executive officer of the company. He returned shortly, relieved
the other law firm, and placed me in charge of the case.

We worked the matter out, and one of the extra benefits was the
impression made on my young partner. He uses the event as an example in speaking about ethics.

What we did was in keeping with the admonition of the American College of Trial Lawyers Code of Trial Conduct that the lawyer
and not the client (which would include co-counsel) is responsible for
decisions as to ethics, and I would include professionalism.

Another example can be seen in a situation I faced in doing an
independent investigation into the E.F. Hutton matter. E.F. Hutton, a
large brokerage company, had pleaded guilty to 2,000 counts of fraud
in the way funds were kited through banks. Hutton was in much trou-
ble with the public and the agencies by which it was regulated. The
problem was made more troubling because the extent of it had never
been determined. It developed that only an insubstantial number of
branch offices had been involved in the questionable conduct.

In our investigation, we were denied many documents on the
advice of Hutton's regular counsel on the basis that their disclosure
would violate the attorney-client privilege. I advised the president of
Hutton that we could not proceed without the documents. I did so
in rather forceful terms by suggesting that Hutton prepare a historical

marker to be placed on the street at the location of their building saying, "Former home of E.F. Hutton, lost while defending the attorney-client privilege." I was making the point that there is such a thing as a Pyrrhic victory. But I was also refusing to do an independent investigation without having all of the pertinent facts. To do otherwise would have been unethical and, to my mind, dishonest.

Another pitfall that awaits lawyers in the modern practice has to do with producing documents. The problem can arise when representing large corporations with thousands of documents at varied locations. In the practice, a lawyer certifies that all documents have been produced, but often the lawyer relies on corporate personnel to produce the documents.

I had the embarrassment of being associated with a failure to produce. In a General Motors case where sanctions were imposed for an unusual delay in producing documents, I was employed to appeal the sanctions order. During oral argument in the Court of Appeals of Georgia, I was asked if all of the documents had finally been produced, and I answered that I understood they had. About the time that the opinion of the court in our favor was rendered, I received notice that some additional documents had been found and were being produced. I had to immediately advise the court of that fact and that my previous statement to the court was incorrect.

The decision of the court stood, but it was a lesson to me and to General Motors. They improved their document production system and I advised our lawyers that we should use a qualifier when certifying, such as "to the best of my knowledge." This is probably the only way that a lawyer can safely engage in document production in representing a large corporation. And this has become an even larger problem in the e-mail age.

There is one last point I would like to make. For lawyers, the obligation of professionalism includes conducting oneself in such a way as to honor the legal profession. We sorely need good citizenship examples, and hardly any are better situated to serve as good examples than lawyers. There is no better way to honor the profession than in honorable conduct, whether in the practice of law or expanded areas of public service. In my opinion, honorable service is the highest calling of a lawyer.

Griffin B. Bell was the 72nd Attorney General of the United States. He served on the Fifth Circuit Court of Appeals from 1961 to 1976. Judge Bell had a long and distinguished legal career until his death, at age 90, on January 5, 2009. Judge Bell joined King & Spalding in 1953 and served as head of the firm's policy committee. At King & Spalding, he served as a lawyer to President George H.W. Bush in the Iran-Contra investigation, led the internal investigation of E.F. Hutton after its plea to 2,000 counts of mail and wire fraud, and headed the internal investigation of Exxon Corporation regarding the grounding of the Exxon Valdez. His list of notable matters is long and distinguished. Judge Bell was a President of the American College of Trial Lawyers and a Lifetime Trustee of Mercer University where he served for many years as Chairman of the Board. He is the author of two books, Taking Care of the Law *and* Footnotes to History. *Judge Bell received numerous awards during his lifetime, but, of all the things he accomplished in his life, he was proudest of the fact that he was a lawyer and practiced what he called the noblest of professions.*

Walking Through the Valley

Timothy W. Floyd

IN 1988, I WAS APPOINTED to represent Louis Jones Jr., who had been sentenced to death for committing an especially terrifying and brutal murder. When I first decided as a young lawyer years ago to take on death-penalty cases, I knew that they came with the harrowing risk that the client might ultimately exhaust all appeals and face execution. That is what happened in the case of Lou Jones. What I never could have anticipated was the personal and spiritual impact that Lou Jones's journey to the death penalty would have on me. When I was appointed, Lou needed my professional help, and as a professional, I gave Lou my best efforts. Over the course of the next seven years, however, I believe I received more in return. The deep paradox is that through my relationship with this man—who had committed an unspeakable act of murder and cruelty—I learned much about pain, grief, remorse, and repentance, but also about faith, hope, and love. Had I not opened myself up on a personal level, I might have spared myself some pain, but I would have missed an unexpected opportunity for spiritual growth.

* * *

It was a Friday in the middle of March 2003, the last day of classes before spring break. My law students were excited about the trips they were taking to the beach, to ski in the mountains, to visit family. I also got on a plane that afternoon, but my destination was the United States Prison in Terre Haute, Indiana. Lou Jones was scheduled to be executed the following Tuesday at 7 a.m. I went to Terre

Haute to attend the likely execution and to be with Lou for what would probably be his last four days. At the same time, however, I was still working to stop this execution.

By March 2003, I had been representing Lou Jones for seven years, through direct appeal in the federal courts, including the United States Supreme Court, and then in post-conviction litigation. The previous November, the Supreme Court had denied certiorari in our post-conviction case, ending hope for a judicial remedy. At that point, the government set an execution date for March 18, 2003, about four months out.

Although we had exhausted all judicial avenues for relief, we did have one executive-level option left: to request that President Bush commute the sentence to one of life without parole. Given President Bush's long record of support for the death penalty and his reluctance to commute any death sentences when he was Governor of Texas, I knew this request was a long shot, to say the least. Nonetheless, I believed that we had solid grounds for a commutation, based on newly discovered evidence that Lou had suffered brain damage due to exposure to Saddam Hussein's nerve gas in the first Gulf War.

During his 22-year Army career, Lou had served with distinction in the United States Army Airborne Rangers in both the Grenada invasion and the first Gulf War. He rose through the ranks to become a Master Sergeant and he was decorated several times. Soon after returning from the Gulf War, he retired with an honorable discharge. But upon returning from the Gulf War, Lou was a changed man; according to his wife, he was hostile, irritable, and rigid. His marriage and his life fell apart. One night in February 1995, in an act of rage and incomprehensible savagery, Lou brutally kidnapped, raped, and murdered a young woman, Private Tracie McBride. Lou never denied his guilt, from the time he was arrested ten days later until his death, and he expressed his profound remorse for what he had done. He was tried in federal court the following autumn, the first case in the nation tried under the Federal Death Penalty Act of 1994.

At his trial, there was no issue as to his guilt; the only question was whether he would receive a sentence of death or of life without possibility of release. Evidence of his exemplary military career and his unblemished record was offered as mitigating evidence to the sentencing jury. The defense also presented testimony of his change in personality after the Gulf War, but they offered no compelling explanation for what could have caused the change in personality. The prosecution relied primarily upon the particular brutality of this crime to urge that he be sentenced to death. The jury struggled in its deliberations for two days, but ultimately sentenced him to death.[1]

Several years after his trial in 1996, the Pentagon admitted that Lou had been exposed to sarin nerve gas in the first Gulf War. Thanks to the work of Dr. Robert Haley, the country's leading expert on Gulf War–related illnesses, we also discovered that he had suffered brain damage as a result of that exposure, brain damage of the type that can lead to the personality and behavior changes that Lou exhibited. It was clear to me that had the jury been aware of that fact, they would more than likely have sentenced Lou to life rather than death. I submitted a detailed Memorandum in Support of Executive Clemency, in which I argued that this was an appropriate case for the President to exercise his constitutional authority to commute the sentence to one of life without possibility of release. I did not know when the President might rule on my request.

The four months between the setting of the execution date and the date itself were the most intense of my life. I had been a lawyer for over 20 years, a professor for much of that time, and I had represented several persons in death-penalty litigation. However, during this time I was playing in a different league, in arenas with which I was not familiar. Executive clemency is more a political process than a legal one, with no controlling standards or precedents.

Nonetheless, we did our best to present a compelling argument to the President. During this time, I made several trips from my home in Lubbock, Texas, to Washington, D.C. I met with White House Counsel Alberto Gonzalez in his office in the West Wing of the White House, and I met with several officials in the United States Department of Justice, including Deputy Attorney General Larry Thompson. Senator Kay Bailey Hutchison of Texas was privately supportive of our efforts, and she ultimately publicly called upon the President to stay the execution. I went to her office on Capitol Hill to meet with her aides. Surprisingly, I even had many conversations with H. Ross Perot, who was actively lobbying for the President to commute Lou's sentence.

These were the months leading up to the invasion of Iraq and a principal basis of the invasion was that Saddam Hussein possessed and was willing to use weapons of mass destruction such as sarin nerve gas.

---

[1] The jury also struggled with instructions that misstated what the sentencing options were in this case. When the United States Supreme Court decided Lou's case in 1999, all nine justices agreed that the jury instructions were in error, but the Court affirmed the conviction in a five-to-four decision. The dissenting justices agreed that the erroneous instructions entitled him to a new sentencing trial.

The media was focused on weapons of mass destruction and on the President's decision to send our troops into Iraq, with every expectation that they would be exposed to nerve gas. The juxtaposition of those events with the evidence of Lou's exposure in the first Gulf War caused our case to receive much more national media attention than any case I had ever worked on. I did not know how to handle the intensity of dealing with the media. I was in over my head and needed help. Fortunately, media consultant Laura Burstein volunteered her time and gave valuable assistance and advice. Our assumption was that too much national publicity would more likely hurt than help our efforts with the President, so we turned down scores of media requests for every one that we granted. Even so, in February and March 2003, I was quoted on the front page of the *New York Times*, was interviewed on National Public Radio, and appeared on *Good Morning America*. Going to the White House and appearing on national television were new experiences for me.

Notwithstanding these frenetic efforts, by March 14, 2003, four days before the scheduled execution, the President had still not ruled on our request. I went to Terre Haute, hoping that the President would spare Lou's life, but in my more realistic moments, I fully expected the execution to go forward.

My feelings as I traveled to Terre Haute were profoundly mixed. I dreaded the likely outcome, but I very much wanted to spend this time with Lou. He was not only my client; he had also become a good friend. Over the past few years, I had spent countless hours with Lou, in person and on the telephone. Most of our conversations were not about the law or his case. Lou had broad interests and read widely— and he loved to talk. After I came to know Lou pretty well, I found myself looking forward to our conversations.

Lou's Christian faith was central to his identity. After his arrest, Lou was visited by a prison ministry, and their work with him led to his conversion to Christianity. While in prison, Lou embraced for himself the promises and the hope of his Christian faith. That faith gave him strength throughout his trial, his time on death row, and in facing his death. Lou and I shared the Christian faith, although we did not always speak about it in the same terms and we certainly did not agree on all theological issues. We did share a deep love for Scripture, and we regularly discussed passages of the Old and New Testaments. When I visited him, we always closed our visits with prayer.

Lou's was not a jailhouse conversion of convenience. His faith was genuine and deep. Once Lou experienced conversion, he sought ways to love others the way he felt loved by God and by the people in the prison ministry. While he was on death row, his cell was near the area where inmates were placed when their execution was imminent. Lou developed a communion ministry for those men to ensure that those facing their last days could experience God's grace and peace.

Through all the intensity of the last four months, Lou remained centered and at peace. Although he did not want to die, Lou was prepared to face death, and he never seemed fearful or anxious. Throughout, though, he was supportive of my efforts and he very much wanted the President to commute his sentence. I am convinced that his biggest concern was leaving his family and friends.

In large part, his peace and courage were the product of his faith. I also suspect, though, that his deep remorse over his brutal crime led him to believe at some level that he deserved to die. In addition, he was not entirely comfortable with my argument in the clemency memorandum; he did not want me to say or write anything on his behalf that suggested he was not responsible for his actions.

In Terre Haute that Saturday, Sunday, and Monday, I spent a good deal of time with Lou, talking and praying (and even laughing on occasion—Lou could always make me laugh). But I was also busy trying to stop this execution: drafting a desperation motion for stay of execution with the United States Supreme Court, talking with the White House Counsel's office, strategizing with Ross Perot, and dealing with the media. Fortunately, I was not alone. Three people from the prison ministry in Texas—Jason Fry, a United Methodist pastor, and Carol Arledge and Irma Brooks, two laywomen—came to Terre Haute to be with Lou. My wife, Daisy, and our 17-year-old son, Will, arrived on Sunday to be with me during these days.

Lou's daughter, Barbara, also arrived for these last days. Barbara was 22 and the mother of two small children. Despite the fact that her father had been in prison since she was 14, they had a close relationship. They spoke regularly on the phone, and Lou continually urged Barbara to do the right thing—stay in school, go to church, pay her bills. It may seem strange, but Lou was a positive moral influence in Barbara's life, and Barbara loved and respected her father very much. Thus, these days were very difficult for her. Barbara was suffering, feeling hopeless, fearful, and angry. She told me that she did not really appreciate "religion talk" about the execution, such as when people said that her dad would be better off in heaven, or that he was going to be with Jesus. Those words did not provide comfort to a young woman about to lose her father.

On Monday afternoon about 4:30, I received a call on my cell phone from Deputy Attorney General Thompson, informing me that the President had denied our request for a commutation.[2] After all our efforts, the execution was going to happen the next morning at 7 o'clock. The first thing I needed to do was tell Barbara, who was in the motel room next door. Then I called the warden, and asked him to try to make sure that Lou did not hear this news until I could come out and tell him in person. A scroll had been running all day on the bottom of the screen on CNN and other networks that our request was being considered by the President. I was concerned that a prison employee might learn about the denial and tell Lou. The warden promised to keep the word from Lou until I could get there.

Barbara decided to wait with Carol and compose herself before she went to see her father. Jason and I went to the prison to break the news to Lou. By this time, it was after 5 p.m., so we were less than 14 hours from the execution. When we told him the news, Lou was a little shaken for a couple of minutes, but he gathered himself quickly. I told him that Barbara would be here soon, and he wanted to get himself together for that. Plainly, he was focused on using his last night on this earth to provide strength to her.

I left when Barbara got there and went back to the motel room. I knew I was not going to sleep that night, but I wanted Barbara to have time alone with her father that evening. I used the next couple of hours to write a statement to be given to the media after the execution. Between 11 and 12, Barbara came back to try to sleep for a couple of hours, so I went back to the prison to be with Lou. From midnight until about 2:30, it was just the two of us, and a remarkable time it was. Lou talked about his childhood, about growing up on the south side of Chicago, and about how he used to hide out in a cemetery from gangs. He talked at length about his mother and the strength and dignity she always demonstrated under very difficult circumstances. We talked about hymns she loved, and I helped him remember the words to one of her favorites: "Jesus Keep Me Near the Cross." We discussed several of his favorite passages of scripture. Lou also talked about the murder in more detail than he ever had with me before; it was clearly weighing on his mind that night. He was haunted by what he had done; senselessly taking the life of such

---

[2] Later that evening, President Bush spoke on national television and gave Saddam Hussein and his sons an ultimatum to leave Iraq or be invaded. Two days later, the war began.

a promising young woman, and causing such anguish for her family and all those who loved her.

I returned to the motel at 2:30 to shower and change. Protocols allowed visitation only until 5 a.m., at which time they would prepare him for the execution. I returned at 4 for a final communion service that Lou and Jason had planned. Barbara, Carol, Jason, and I, along with two prison chaplains, were in the tiny visitation space outside Lou's cell. Lou was on the other side of the glass. Although we could not have physical contact with Lou, we could hear each other. Jason presided over the communion liturgy and we shared communion wafers and grape juice. At the close of the service, Jason asked if anyone wished to pray, and we went around the circle, each one of us whispering a prayer. When the prayers moved at last to Lou, he stood and placed both hands on the glass, looked up, smiled, and said, "This is the day the Lord has made, let us rejoice and be glad in it."

What a gift. Lou's message to us was that he was ready. His expression of faith and trust that morning, when his own life would be ended in a couple of hours, profoundly moved us all. Barbara later told my daughter, Kate, that for the first time she felt the presence of peace about these events.

All of us except Barbara left immediately after the communion service. Barbara remained with her father from 4:30 until 5, saying their final goodbyes. Lou and Barbara had earlier agreed that she would not attend the execution itself, so at 5 prison officials took Barbara from the prison back to the motel where she would spend the hours surrounding the execution with my wife and son.

At a few minutes before 7 a.m., the four of us who were there to witness the execution on Lou's behalf were taken to the witness room. We sat in chairs facing a curtain. Just as we were getting settled, the curtains were opened. Lou was on the gurney facing us with a white sheet covering him to his neck. The sheet covered the IV that was in his arm, but I could see a tube running through a hole in the wall to a room out of our sight, from where the deadly poison would come. An official with the Bureau of Prisons and a United States Marshall were in the room with Lou on either side of the gurney. Lou was able to see us and we were able to see him. He couldn't hear us, but there was a microphone in the execution chamber that allowed us to hear everything that was said in the death chamber.

Looking one by one at each of the four of us, he said "I love you." Very quickly after that, the prison official read the sentence as entered by the Judge and stated that the sentence would now be carried out. The official asked Lou if he had a final statement to make. He recited in a strong clear voice a verse from Psalm 118: "The Lord hath chastened me sore: but he hath not given me over unto death." (The night before, Lou had written out a final statement in which he once more expressed his remorse over the pain, anguish, and suffering he had caused the McBrides. However, he did not want a Bureau of Prisons official whom he did not know reading his final words. He had slipped that piece of paper to me earlier that morning and asked me to read it to the media after the execution, which I did.)

He then began to sing the hymn "Jesus Keep Me Near the Cross." (Now I knew why he wanted help in remembering those words.) He started with the chorus: "In the cross, in the cross, be my glory ever 'til my raptured soul shall find rest beyond the river." I cannot say that he sang well, but he sang out quite strongly. He then sang the first verse and repeated the chorus. He kept singing even as the chemicals were injected into his body and his lips grew forever still. After he finished the chorus the second time, finishing with the words "rest beyond the river," he stopped singing. His eyes were wide open but his face became still. His lips were half-parted as if halted in mid-song. I was looking at his chest and it was clear that he was no longer breathing. He was pronounced dead a few minutes later. The curtains then closed and we were hustled out.

Immediately after the execution, the government scheduled press conferences. First, the prosecutor and the victim's family met the press and answered questions. The Assistant United States Attorney who had prosecuted the case told the reporters that, in light of the impending war, a lawyer who would use evidence of Gulf War illness to try to help Louis Jones was "despicable." Her words would be in newspapers throughout the country the next day—the day that the United States invaded Iraq. I did not feel much like facing the press, but I needed to read Lou's final statement as I had promised. Jason and I also made our own statements and answered questions.

Two days later, the community who had gathered in Terre Haute for the execution gathered in Chicago for Lou's funeral. Our daughter, Kate, and Jason's wife and children came to Chicago from Texas, and several of Lou's siblings also attended. Barbara embodied remarkable grace and dignity while hosting and reconciling all those who were there. The funeral was a powerful and moving service of remembrance of Lou and, for me, affirmed my faith that nothing can separate us from the love of God. Lou was buried in a cemetery on the south side of Chicago, the same cemetery in which he had hidden as a boy.

Seeing the government's machinery of death—up close and personal—confirmed and strengthened my opposition to capital punishment and renewed my commitment to abolish it. The death-penalty system shows our criminal justice system at its worst. The process for determining who receives death is rife with arbitrariness, bias, and unfairness and with political posturing and unprincipled decision-making. We do not have a system that fairly and even-handedly singles out those most deserving of the ultimate punishment—and I am convinced that we are not capable of creating such a system.

I have gained a better understanding of success in the practice of law. Ours is an adversarial legal system, and it is easy to define our value as lawyers in terms of winning and losing. By that measure, I certainly "lost" Lou's case, but I do not believe I was a failure. As advocates, our responsibility is not to win every case. Our calling is to be faithful to our clients, even when the odds appear overwhelming. Make no mistake, I am still very frustrated at the process and the outcome, and the result still haunts me. There are many of us who miss Lou and see his death as a waste. There was much good he could have done had he been allowed to serve out his days in federal prison.

My experience with Louis Jones has given me a new appreciation for the importance of relationships. Our popular image of trial lawyers, especially criminal defense lawyers, is that of the lonely champion standing alone at the side of his or her client. But good lawyering cannot be done alone. Starting with the individualistic nature of law school, new lawyers receive the message that lawyers work alone and must rely solely on their own knowledge, skill, and judgment. Although my name was the only one on the clemency application, I had help from many people who gave tremendous amounts of time, all as volunteers (including most prominently Dick Burr, who has dedicated his life to the defense of capital defendants; Dick is one of the finest lawyers and persons I have ever known). People who do death-penalty defense work often refer to the death-penalty defense "community"; that word is entirely accurate and descriptive. I have rarely encountered a more supportive and helpful group of people.

My family was also indispensable. I had planned to go to Terre Haute alone for the execution. After all, I anticipated that Daisy would not be allowed into the prison so I believed that there was not much she would be able to do there. Daisy knew better. She chose to go in order to be with and support me. In retrospect, I cannot imagine how I would have handled it without her presence, her wisdom, and her strength. It was also a blessing that Daisy and Will were there for Barbara during the execution itself. They were a great comfort to her during those early morning hours. I am embarrassed to admit that I had not thought ahead of time about where Barbara would be or who she would be with during the execution; I hate to think that she might have been alone at that time. I also still marvel at the little community that gathered in Terre Haute to be with Lou and each other during those days. Jason and Carol and Irma had not known each other before these events brought them together, and they had little in common, other than their deep faith and desire to be there in love and faith for Lou and for Barbara.

In death-penalty defense work, there is a natural human temptation to ignore or minimize the awful things our clients have done. It is a mistake, however, to turn a blind eye to the horrific nature of our clients' crimes. Sister Helen Prejean often reminds us that each of us is worth more than the worst thing that we have ever done. That is certainly true of Louis Jones—there was much that was good in him. He served his country honorably and courageously for over 20 years as a United States Army Airborne Ranger; he was a devoted father and grandfather to Barbara and her two children; he was a man of deep faith who had a positive impact on many of those around him, including while he was on death row. I focused on these things in my relationship with Lou and in my advocacy for him.

Still, I must face the fact that the worst thing that Lou Jones did was truly horrible. Lou never stopped dwelling on his awful crime, including during his last night. When Lou was executed, his own daughter, whom he loved desperately, was close to the age of Tracie McBride when he murdered her. Indeed, my own daughter Kate, who means the world to me, was also very close to that same age. When I remember Lou, there is always a part of me that remembers with horror his brutal and senseless crime. I cannot imagine the pain that the McBride family will always feel.

I came into Lou's life as his attorney, and that remained the fundamental feature of our relationship. I could have done a good job as his lawyer without developing a personal friendship with him. But we did become friends, and I do not regret that friendship. I've come to believe that keeping "professional distance" from clients is overrated. I fully appreciate the need for boundaries and objectivity, for not letting judgment become clouded by feelings. We lawyers, however, often invoke the legitimate need for professional distance as a justification for not "getting too close" to our clients. Many lawyers are afraid of getting close to their clients, especially when there is so much at stake. A couple of criminal defense lawyers whom I know suggested to me that I was too close to Lou. But I do not regret my relationship with Lou Jones, and I do not believe that it adversely affected my representation of him.

The execution may have been more difficult for me than it would have been had I not been Lou's friend, although watching as the government kills one's client would be very difficult in any event. But even if the execution was more painful, I also caught glimpses of redemption and hope that I would not have seen if I had not allowed Lou into my life. Because I became his friend, I knew at a deep level this man's remorse and repentance, and his faith, his hope, and his love. Loss is more painful the closer we are to the person, but that is no reason not to get close. Indeed, it has only been through fully embracing these events at a deep emotional level that I have been able to cope and move forward in my life.

In representing Louis Jones, I learned much about being a lawyer. I learned even more about life and faith and hope and grace.

Professor Timothy W. Floyd is a Professor of Law and Director of the Law and Public Service Program at Mercer University's Walter F. George School of Law. He received his B.A. and M.A. degrees from Emory University and his law degree from the University of Georgia. After clerking with Judge Phyllis A. Kravitch on the Eleventh Circuit Court of Appeals and a term in private practice at Sutherland, Asbill & Brennan, in 1992, Professor Floyd began his law school teaching career at the University of Georgia, teaching later at Texas Tech University School of Law before joining the faculty at Mercer. Professor Floyd is widely published on issues of ethics, law and religion, and the death penalty.

Serving the Public

Robert B. Fiske Jr.

TWO OF THE MOST IMPORTANT obligations of every lawyer are to make a meaningful contribution to public service—country, state, or local community—and to make a meaningful contribution to the professional development of the younger lawyers he or she works with.

Both of these principles became clear to me at the start of my career. As a second-year law student at the University of Michigan, I spent the summer of 1954 working as a student assistant in the United States Attorney's Office for the Southern District of New York. I saw firsthand the tremendous influence the United States Attorney, J. Edward Lumbard (later to become the Chief Judge of the Second Circuit Court of Appeals), had on the development and training of the Assistant United States Attorneys who worked for him (I have spent my whole career following his admonition to "never assume a damn thing") and the strong motivation he instilled in them to make public service an important part of their careers.

He was a mentor and a role model for scores of young lawyers, including me, and I am indebted to him and to two of my partners in private practice at Davis Polk: Hazard Gillespie (United States Attorney and New York State Bar President) and Lawrence Walsh (United States District Judge, Deputy Attorney General, and Iran-Contra Independent Counsel) for the development of my professional skills. Working with them—learning by instruction as well as example— I learned firsthand how valuable and important mentoring from a senior lawyer is to the development, growth, and morale of those starting their legal careers.

When I became the United States Attorney in 1976, one of the
most exciting aspects of the position was the opportunity to influence
the professional training and the development of important values in
the outstanding group of young lawyers who pursued the opportunity to work in the United States Attorney's office at the outset of
their careers. I devoted significant time to direct interpersonal contact with each one of them—discussing strategy in their cases, watching them in their court appearances, and in many cases "teaching by
doing" in the handling of important cases personally. One of the most
gratifying aspects of my career has been to watch that group of 28- to
30-year-old lawyers become leaders of the bar, managing partners in
major New York law firms, general counsels of major U.S. corporations, and holders of significant positions in public service, including
Attorney General of the United States, federal judges and state judges,
United States Attorney for the Southern District of New York, and
general counsel of the CIA. Since leaving the office, 50 of these former Assistant United States Attorneys have devoted substantial por-
tions of their careers to public service—including full-time positions
in the federal, state, or city government or as participants in various
independent counsel investigations on the federal, state, or city level.

Similarly in private practice, one of the principal reasons I am
still practicing law as an active partner at age 78 is because of the
stimulation that comes from working directly on major cases with
younger lawyers in the firm and having the same kind of opportunity to advance their professional skills and ethical values that I did
with the Assistant United States Attorneys in the Southern District.
My law firm is very proud of its tradition of public service, and a
number of the associates I have worked with have gone on to become
federal judges, members of Congress, and have held important positions in federal, state, and city government.

One important value I have tried to impress on every lawyer—
young and old—with whom I have worked is civility. A federal
prosecutor—or a lawyer in private practice—can be hard-hitting
and aggressive without being unpleasant or difficult to deal with. An
equally important value, and one that I tried to make a hallmark of
the United States Attorney's Office while I was there, is fairness to
subjects of a criminal investigation. That means among other things,
no leaks to the press about an ongoing investigation—ideally if the
investigation resulted in a decision not to prosecute, the public should
never know it existed. In the case of one public official in which
the investigation had become known, putting him under a cloud,

we agreed with his counsel that fairness dictated that the official be sent a letter when the investigation was concluded stating that no wrongdoing had been found. While serving as Independent Counsel in the Whitewater investigation, we had several discussions within the office about whether to serve a grand jury subpoena on an institution calling for the production of documents relating to a number of individuals. While we were confident that we were entitled to the information, we knew the names of the individuals would become public, thereby inevitably damaging their reputations. We decided to withhold serving the subpoenas until we had fully satisfied ourselves that we could not obtain the necessary information in some other way. In the end, we were not going to compromise the ability of our office to obtain all the relevant information—that was a sine qua non—but we were determined to try to do it, if we could, in a way that would not jeopardize individuals' reputations.

Implicit—indeed foremost—in the mentoring and training of younger lawyers is the installation of the highest principles of ethical conduct. That is taught in the most valuable way by what younger lawyers learn from watching the decision-making process in actual situations as they occur. One very specific example is a case we had several years ago in which our client was being sued in New York by a foreign company. Based on all the facts we knew at the time, we made a motion to dismiss the case on grounds of forum non conveniens, arguing that none of the alleged wrongful conduct had occurred in this country. While the motion was pending, we learned of certain conduct—which was not in the record before the Court, and was unknown to our adversary, but was inconsistent with the argument we had made to the Court. After discussions among ourselves, we concluded we had no choice but to withdraw the motion, which (without disclosing the reason) we did.

What we do as lawyers requires us to remember that we are professionals, that integrity is the watchword of how we practice, and, in the end, these are the values we must pass along to those who follow us. Without this focus, our profession is diminished in the eyes of the public and even among us as members of the bar.

Robert B. Fiske Jr. is a senior member of Davis Polk & Wardwell's Litigation Department, where he specializes in professional liability, securities, products liability, and white-collar crime cases. He was the United States Attorney for the Southern District of New York from 1976 to 1980. As United States Attorney, Mr. Fiske served as Chairman of the Attorney General's Advisory Committee of United States Attorneys. He served as Independent Counsel in the Whitewater Investigation from January to August 1994.

Mr. Fiske has served as chairman of a Judicial Commission on Drugs and the Courts, appointed by New York State Chief Judge Judith S. Kaye. He also was a member of the Commission for the Review of FBI Security Programs (Webster Commission). He is a former President of the American College of Trial Lawyers.

CHAPTER 11

On Encouraging Civility

Honorable William S. Duffey Jr.

I REMEMBER THAT AFTERNOON too well. I was the lead partner in a particularly difficult case—a commercial dispute between parties competing hard in a tough industry. The stakes were high and the clients demanded successful results. It was important to them. The lawyers on the other side were aggressive and, in my view, unreasonable. The litigation environment was unpleasant and nerves were frayed as we entered the last weeks of discovery.

The issue that afternoon was the scheduling and scope of a Rule 30(b)(6) deposition. The scheduling discussions were not going well. A younger lawyer from the opposing firm was charged with resolving this issue for his client, and he had to deal with me. He was at most a mid-level associate, and he had not been especially active in the litigation. Our client was being hard-nosed on this scheduling, and I had not enjoyed dealing with him on it. He insisted we resist what opposing counsel wanted at all costs. I was frustrated and my nerves were shot when my young adversary called to try to put this scheduling issue to rest. I resisted everything he suggested, probably for the sake of resisting. I remember being uncooperative and unpleasant. Then he said something that just struck me the wrong way. I do not recall that the comment was rude or angry, just that it did not sit well. I let loose with what I am sure was received as an intemperate lecture to a young lawyer who was simply trying to do his best to deal with a difficult issue. While I hate to admit it now, I cut the conversation short and left the issue open.

As I got some distance from the conversation, I found myself wondering why it was so upsetting to me. In a moment of honest reflection, I realized how disappointed I was in myself. The more I replayed the conversation over in my mind, the more I recognized that I was not upset about failing to seek resolution to the issue but about how I had behaved. The more I considered the conversation, the more I regretted how I had treated a younger colleague who simply was given the assignment to do his best to resolve an issue.

I would like to say I acted immediately, but it took longer than it should have to make the call. I remember how tentative my young opponent was when he answered the phone, probably fearing he was in for more of the same from me. While I cannot remember our whole conversation, I remember two things very clearly. First, I told him plainly and unequivocally that I was sorry for how I had acted, and that I did not have any excuse for how I had treated him in our conversation. I told him that I knew I was impeding our ability to get beyond an issue we both needed to settle. I also told him that one of the things I had regretted about our profession was the increasing acrimony that was evident among lawyers in litigation. And then I told him that I hoped he would remember my role in the conversation as a reminder of how not to act.

There is one other time I wish I had kept my tongue in check. I was involved in a matter after I became responsible for the United States Attorney's Office in Atlanta. We were prosecuting a case against a law enforcement agency employee who had disclosed confidential information that put other law enforcement officers and their investigative strategies at risk. The employee's actions were egregious, and he had been indicted for it. We were discussing with his lawyer the terms on which he might enter a plea. We were near the end of the negotiations, and the focus was on the term of imprisonment the defendant should face. His lawyer and I disagreed about what was appropriate. When I stated my view of a reasonable plea, the defense lawyer responded with a sarcastic, inappropriate attack on our office, our integrity, and me personally. I responded with several terse, biting remarks, and the meeting ended abruptly.

Within minutes after the meeting concluded, I thought about what had occurred. I, and the other lawyers from my office who were with me, all agreed that my response was justified, that we had been provoked, and that the defense lawyer was way out of line. While I concurred in their assessment, I knew it was my job to create an environment where we could explore whether his client might plead to his offense. I knew I had to call the defense lawyer and schedule another meeting. We reconvened a few days later. I began by apologizing for my reaction during our prior meeting and we both acknowledged that we needed to get past our last conversation to determine whether we could agree on a reasonable plea agreement to conclude the matter. Within a very short time, an agreement was struck.

These are two very different examples. Thinking back on these two incidents, I know that my decision to reconcile these relationships was professionally, and personally, important. In the first, the conduct I modeled for my younger colleague was wrong. At that stage in my career, it was my responsibility to exhibit professionalism—grace under fire. If I could do that, I could at least model my willingness to make amends. In the second incident, I realized that in life there will be times when we are justified to act as we do. The question is whether our actions, while justified, are right. In my encounter with this defense counsel, I decided my public function required me to consider the interests of justice and the defendant's desire to accept responsibility for the crime that he had committed. It was irresponsible for me to allow his lawyer to interfere with my duty to serve justice, even if circumstances "justified" my response. My ultimate decision in these two instances was to model professionalism to a young lawyer and to serve our justice system in a responsible way. These values prompted me to make two very difficult telephone calls. The calls simply were the right response to my errors in judgment.

The work we do is hard. The pressure is often intense, and the demands unreasonable. None of these excuse impulsive, intemperate conduct. Ours is a profession of service to others and to clients. We are charged with addressing and resolving tough issues that often have important and substantial consequences. The incivility and hostility of litigation today not only makes this work more unpleasant, less satisfying, and less fulfilling, but it also serves as a barrier to what we are charged to do—to represent clients in the resolution of disputes by seeking just results. My conduct was a barrier, in both of these examples, to the service to our profession and the public. There will be times in one's professional life when an apology is in order because of the way we have treated someone in a case. Making the call to express your regret is hard. You have to swallow your pride and risk the vulnerability of admitting you were wrong. But it will be a necessary step to restore professional and personal relationships with another lawyer so progress in a case can be made and a resolution achieved. That is our duty: to seek justice and to treat others with dignity.

William S. Duffey Jr. is a United States District Judge for the Northern District of Georgia. Prior to taking the bench, Judge Duffey served as United States Attorney in Atlanta. He had previously served as Deputy Independent Counsel in charge of the Arkansas phase of the Whitewater Investigation. Before his current tour in public service, Judge Duffey had a distinguished career as a litigator in private practice. Judge Duffey graduated with honors from Drake University in 1973 and graduated cum laude in 1977 from the University of South Carolina School of Law.

On Autonomy and Professionalism
Ralph B. Levy

FROM 1993 THROUGH 1999 I served as managing partner of a major Atlanta law firm. It was my custom to welcome young, new equity partners with advice regarding the relationship between how they manage their personal financial affairs and the autonomy a lawyer needs to be able to exercise appropriate judgment. I entreated them to treat their colleagues fairly, to take care of the long-term interests of the law firm, and to enjoy a satisfying career. I "preached" this message because I believe the way one lives their personal life is directly tied to how they act professionally. That is, living life in a financially reasonable way allows a lawyer the freedom to provide objective advice and judgment without the pressure to create income to fund a life too fully leveraged financially. The end goal of my advice to younger lawyers was to encourage them to maintain their personal, financial, and professional independence, because that is what is required for a lawyer to engage in the practice of law successfully and to service clients fully.

The need for independence and objectivity are the underpinnings of the professionalism movement in law that was developing when I began my "sermons" to our incoming equity partners. They are critical values to which lawyers must adhere. Without it lawyers are influenced by pressures and influences that cause us to treat each other and our system of justice in a way that erodes public confidence—including ours—in the legal profession. The need to address this erosion was recognized by our courts two decades ago.

In the late 1980s and early 1990s states, like mine, began to focus on professionalism, as distinguishable from ethics, to address the concern that lawyers have lost their way in terms of courtesy and civility; that our focus has concentrated on income rather than our profession.

Scores have been written about the theoretical distinction between legal ethics, on the one hand, and lawyer professionalism, on the other hand. The distinction usually focuses on the former as a codification of a set of situation-specific rules of conduct. Professionalism promotes a transcending "Golden Rule" for lawyers. Some definitional debate persists, but many lawyers intuitively understand the difference between ethics and professionalism. Some don't appreciate and may not care much about the differences. Regrettably, real progress in meeting the goal of increased courtesy and civility on a widespread basis remains elusive. While most lawyers would probably agree that courtesy and civility are worthy and noble, they also would likely agree, based on their experience in the trenches, that behavior has not much improved since professionalism became a mandatory continuing legal education (CLE) requirement. The question is, why not?

We recognize there are four fundamental premises of lawyer professionalism: autonomy, loyalty to client, maintaining confidentiality of client information, and vigorous client representation. I believe the last three of these lawyer professionalism premises are generally honored, not only by lawyers who are routinely courteous and civil, but even by those who are not. That lawyers on both ends of the civility/courtesy continuum generally carry out their duties of client loyalty, confidentiality, and vigorous representation is hardly surprising. These basic premises are valued, not only by proponents of professionalism, but perhaps more importantly, they are valued and demanded by clients. Lawyers who regularly fail to honor them confront the very practical risk of losing business. Client expectations alone might be adequate to continue to instill these values, even without the bar requiring CLE courses in professionalism. I suspect there remains a role for CLE training in this area, but only to reinforce these values.

What is missing, in my view, is an adequate set of practical processes to instill and provoke lawyer autonomy, which ironically is the first foundational premise of professionalism. Unlike the other three values, which clients regularly enforce even by malpractice litigation if necessary, I do not recall a client encouraging me to be autonomous.

Indeed, clients often want to dictate the direction and frequently the decisions of a lawyer in a legal matter. Autonomy is degraded in other ways. Sometimes it comes from the pressure of other lawyers to implement a certain legal tactic to accommodate the client who is, after all, paying the bills. Oftentimes it is the pressure for job security, a steady income to fund personal commitments and lifestyle. Whether it is client control, pressure from practicing colleagues, or personal financial demands—each interferes with the ability to act objectively in representing a client. The erosion of autonomy from each influence is real. I believe the pressure a lawyer feels when his or her independence is challenged often is manifested in uncivil and discourteous behavior toward others in the profession. There must be an influence to encourage a lawyer to guard against this erosion of independence and autonomy. It will lead, I believe, to independence, from which will flow civil, professional conduct.

The professionalism movement, in our profession, is not merely a reinforcing influence respecting lawyer autonomy—it may be the only influence that encourages a lawyer's autonomy, absent a respected personal mentor to guide the lawyer along his professional way. The professionalism movement might be expected to enjoy spotty success if its emphasis is on values that are already largely enforced by clients. What we need is autonomy—a key value about which clients are relatively indifferent and sometimes antagonistic. In my view, there is a lot at stake—including how we function as a profession and the self-regulation that has been entrusted to us. More implicitly, satisfaction in the practice of law degrades if professionalism erodes. The evidence is clear.

Independence has always been a key component in the profession's claim to the privilege of self-regulation. Professionalism's allusion to a Golden Rule makes sense only if lawyers are intellectually free to follow it, which means that countervailing financial or other pressures must be understood for what they are and subordinated to the value of doing the right thing. Moreover, in addition to the unfortunate role that incivility and discourtesy play in the public's unfavorable impression of lawyers (as evidenced by the ubiquitous lawyer jokes), the health and well-being of those who labor within the profession may be adversely affected by an environment in which the Golden Rule is honored more in the breach than in the observance. It has recently been reported: "That lawyers are among the most miserable of men—and women—is well known. Some 19 percent of lawyers suffer depression at any given time, compared with

6.7 percent of the population as a whole . . . and one in five lawyers is a problem drinker, twice the national rate."[1]

Professionalism concerns arise and the personal satisfaction that should accompany the practice of law declines when we behave as if there is an inconsistency between business interests, on the one hand, and the interests of courtesy and civility to opposing counsel and the courts, on the other hand, and vigorous representation is distorted to corrosive extremes. That there is no inconsistency in fact that supports such behavior should not be debatable. Some of the most successful and satisfied lawyers I know are also shining lights of professionalism. These lawyers realize that they can offer all manner of professional courtesies, even when they are not responded to in kind, yet maintain the complete confidence of their clients and trounce their opponents handily on the merits. It is not that those who behave otherwise are irrational. Rather, it seems that the muscular independence enjoyed by prior generations has atrophied largely as a result of pressures, mostly financial pressures, which are relatively new to the practice of law.

Historically the profession, when practiced ably, offered the prospect of a satisfying life supported by a more-than-decent earned income. Prior generations of lawyers expected to do well but to practice fairly late into their productive lives to accommodate retirement. The notion, aided and abetted by transparency of financial results reported in the legal media, that the law profession can and should broadly allow for the creation of wealth is a relatively new idea, however. Even more recent is the idea that the profession can accommodate retirement after a relatively short career.

As these new ideas were forming, and perhaps as a consequence of their allure, the historical stability of practice groups became something that could no longer be taken for granted. The frequency and velocity of partner lateral movements and even partner de-equitizations have become subjects of daily comment in the legal media. Many law firms have abandoned or substantially reduced partner retirement plans, leaving partners to their own devices for retirement planning but without the assurance of partnership tenure. It might be a mere coincidence that the professionalism movement began at about the same time that these developments were taking hold and gaining momentum, but I doubt it. Surely there

---

[1] Sue Shellenbarger, *Lawyers More Willing to Take On Depression,* THE ATLANTA JOURNAL-CONSTITUTION, December 19, 2007, at C3.

must be an unwelcome consequence if the rewards expected from the profession are materially increasing while law firm security is decreasing and the clients' view of the value of lawyer work remains constant. The profession cannot easily accommodate such change except for a relative few, and the competition to be counted among the relative few has become overheated.

The relationship between lawyer and client is also becoming more fickle and civility suffers when lawyers believe that their client relationship is at stake. Lawyers can reasonably expect that as a consequence of higher pricing—justified by higher associate salaries or other costs, the desire for higher firm profits, or both—that failing to achieve the client's objective will more frequently result in loss of client business. Such pressure makes it more difficult for opposing lawyers to reach cordial accommodation even on matters that are relatively trivial.

It is possible that the profession will be forced to self-correct in time. Many of the most recent law school graduates are rejecting these pressures. It seems that no matter how high starting salaries go, some associates, including some among the most highly qualified, lack partnership aspirations and leave the profession for quality-of-life reasons once their student debt is brought under control. The profession may be forced to adopt an entirely new model if the best and the brightest reject its allure in large enough numbers. But between now and then, the professionalism movement has a significant role to play to encourage lawyer autonomy in the face of such pressures.

Autonomy, the state of mind in which professionalism thrives, suffers if one's financial needs or expectations are heightened to a point where the loss of a single case or a busted deal fuels crisis. It is human nature to behave badly under such pressure. Keynes wrote that "[t]he love of money as a possession—as distinguished from the love of money as a means to the enjoyments and realities of life—will be recognized for what it is, a somewhat disgusting morbidity, one of those semi-criminal, semi-pathological propensities which one hands over with a shudder to the specialists in mental disease."[2] Is there any real doubt that professional courtesy would be materially enhanced if we were to arrive in the office each morning because we enjoy what we do rather than because we have left ourselves no choice? Those whose lives are so highly leveraged that they have to

---

[2] JOHN MAYNARD KEYNES, ESSAYS IN PERSUASION [1931], pt. V.

bill many hours a day to survive impose an "incivility tax" on those with whom they deal.

We are all the product of our personal experiences. My father came to maturity just in time for the Great Depression. Like others of his generation, his experience resulted in a lifelong aversion to debt. He was successful nonetheless and his family wanted for nothing, but what we received, including our home, was only acquired if it could be purchased for cash. For him, the absence of undue financial pressure and peace of mind went hand in glove. (I can't imagine how much sleep he must have lost worrying about my first home purchase at the mid-teen mortgage rates that prevailed in the 1970s!) While I did not avoid debt to quite the same extreme, I was driven by my legacy to pay it off as quickly as possible even in low-interest-rate periods when it did not necessarily make economic or tax sense to do so. Being without financial pressure for a large portion of one's career is a wonderful thing. The resulting freedom is enabling. It is easier to apply the Golden Rule and otherwise do what you think is right. In my view, the freedom benefit more than offsets the opportunity cost. Not everyone will make the same value judgment. Others may be intellectually strong enough to maintain professional autonomy even in the face of financial pressure. But I suspect professionalism would improve materially if more of us thought seriously about the trade-offs.

My perspective affected how I related to newly elected partners during my tenure as managing partner of my large law firm in the 1990s. After imparting well-earned congratulations, I would say something like this:

> We are in the institution-building business. You have been elected to join us because we believe that, through your efforts, the firm will continue to grow and prosper, as it must to afford opportunities to those who come behind you, which is what institutions are all about. Your rewards cannot come from "pulling up the ladder." We need to make the firm richer and you will prosper as a consequence. But you will be a far better colleague and partner, and will be able to support long-term investments for the future, which may not pay off in your own time, if you calibrate your success in terms of the firm's long-term success. To be free to do that, avoid the temptation to upwardly adjust your lifestyle with each and every increase in your partner percentage share. I hope you make a lot of money during your time at the firm, but I also hope that you do not need or want to spend it all. Draw some

reasonable expenditure line in the sand and prudently invest the excess. You will be happier. Uneven cash flows and even the inevitable "down year" will not produce crisis in your life. And years from now, if you want to slow down or alter your practice mix to reduce the pressures of an increasingly competitive profession, you will have the financial freedom to make an accommodation that is mutually fair to yourself and the firm. You will continue to come to the office because you want to, not because you have to, and making your firm better than before you joined it can take priority in your life.

Some listened; some probably didn't. I suspect those that did and acted on the suggestion are better off for it and enjoy the autonomy that is necessary to routinely apply the Golden Rule to both their colleagues and their adversaries. I also suspect the suggestion is needed now more than ever if, or precisely because, the current response to such a message might frequently be: "What world does this guy live in?" My answer: a far better one in which courtesy and civility provide the lubricant for career satisfaction and enjoyment to subsist alongside very long hours and very hard work.

Admittedly, the attitude that "firm comes first" is a harder sell in a relatively new environment in which partners aspire to change firms, sometimes on multiple occasions. Many of those changes occur, in my view, when the centrifugal force of personal financial gratification becomes disproportionate to the centripetal force of loyalty to existing colleagues and firm to jointly build together from within. The full effect over the long term of the failure to maintain equipoise between these forces is unknown but undoubtedly threatening to lawyer institutions and core values including professionalism. It may even be a precursor of worse things to come: "It has been said that a nation without ideals cannot long survive. Neither can our profession."[3]

Make no mistake. I am certainly not arguing that lawyers should take some kind of penurious oath. To the contrary, values that I hold dear, including firm building for future generations and enhanced diversity in our profession, all require significant ambition, keen competitiveness, and material financial success. What bothers me is that we can achieve all of that without abandoning the muscular autonomy, the fierce professional independence from the client

---

[3] Wm. Reece Smith, Jr., *Professionalism? What's That?*, FLA. BAR J. (May 1998).

or the client's cause, which allows the best among us to do battle, sometimes pitched battle, within a framework of civility, courtesy, and mutual respect, a framework in which the "enemy" is an opposing position or idea, not opposing counsel or the court. I am suggesting that lawyers who find it difficult regularly to be among the "best" in this sense should carefully examine whether forces in their lives, personal financial forces in particular, are getting in the way of professional behavior. Simply understanding what is occurring may be of behavior-changing assistance. Or honest reflection and self-assessment may suggest that a recalibration of some kind is required.

Why should lawyers, who generally believe in and aspire to excellence in so many facets of their careers, accept anything less in their professional dealings with each other? Something is getting in the way. Either we have lost our sense of the fundamental rightness of autonomy, the critical premise that to zealously represent our clients we have no need to be defined by them or their causes in our own professional relationships, or our ability effectively to adhere to the right. Continuing legal education in professionalism would do well to place considerably more emphasis on such concerns, for our autonomy hygiene seems in need of a boost.

Ralph B. Levy is a Senior Partner in the Atlanta office of King & Spalding LLP, where he served for seven years as its Managing Partner. Mr. Levy is a business litigator who currently serves as a sought-after mediator and arbitrator of business and professional disputes. He is an authority on issues of legal ethics, and is the driving force behind the Atlanta Large Law Firm Diversity Alliance. Mr. Levy graduated cum laude from Lehigh University in 1967 and was a cum laude graduate from the University of Pennsylvania Law School in 1970. Mr. Levy is the 2007 recipient of the Equal Opportunity Award presented by the Women and Minorities in the Profession Committee of the State Bar of Georgia.

CHAPTER 13

Keeping Perspective—
The Value of Relationships
Karen P. Tandy

Dearest Thelma (or you can be Louise if you feel strongly about it)—Cannot imagine my life without you . . . it would be like a symphony orchestra that is missing the violin section. So, my dearest friend since at least 7th grade . . . don't go anywhere without me. You complete me. You are the bold, daring, courageous part of me that I could only hope to be but never could quite let go of the reins long enough to experience. I will treasure this week's all too brief moments when we got to relive being silly, high school girls. Although, I am quite certain that you got even funnier with age. I don't lament the years that I stupidly let pass without you because I cannot do anything about that now. . . . I just rejoice that God repositioned our chess pieces and put us together again. I love you, Thelma. Louise (December 27, 2007)

This e-mail two days after Christmas in 2007 says it all. I love my friend "Thelma." Thelma is not her real name any more than Louise is mine. But, the bond of Hollywood's "Thelma and Louise" fits us. My dear friend Thelma loves life. She is crazy, guileless, adorable, and loves to make people laugh. To the casual observer, we were the least likely to find each other in junior high school and perhaps even less likely to remain bonded throughout life—from high school and college, through marriage and children, and the decades of communication gaps that evaporated each time we saw each other. Quite simply, we were meant to be.

From age 13, we were the odd couple—she was artistic, popular, gorgeous, and petite. More than half a foot taller, I was the bookworm, struggling with "bad hair," yo-yo dieting, and all the standard teenage insecurities. Despite our physical differences, we were

one. We were inseparable, driving endlessly around a parking lot—
our teenage hangout—every Friday night in her Mustang sports car,
slathering on baby oil laced with iodine to achieve the perfect tan,
working our first summer jobs together at an amusement park, and
buying a puppy with our generous $1.40 hourly wages, all part of an
ill-fated plan to add the creature to our small college dorm room.
And, as good friends do, we picked up the pieces for each other during the tough times of youth—the innumerable romantic breakups,
lost contests, and searches for new goals.

Then, our lives went in opposite directions—entering marriage
and bearing children more than a decade apart, and pursuing differ-
ing career paths, hers inside the home and mine on the outside with
moves that took me 1,600 miles away. We lost touch for many years.
It would have been so easy to close that chapter in our lives, to mark
it "the early years." How many times have we unexpectedly encountered old friends, only to find that there is nothing to talk about after
the perfunctory "catch-up" questions, or avoided eye contact with
people altogether to avoid the artificial chat and pregnant pauses?
That was me. I never went to any of our high school reunions, not
even the big ones. I reasoned, "After all this time, what could we possibly have in common to talk about?" Nothing, I was quite certain.

With Thelma, it was different. Although we had grown apart in
our adult lives, we had not fundamentally changed from the girls we
were when we first found each other in seventh grade. More than
sharing a short history growing up together, we shared a connected-
ness. Thelma was my touchstone. We were meant to be. I reached out
to Thelma at every major turn in my life—my wedding, the birth
of my children, and my swearing-in ceremony as the Administrator
of the Drug Enforcement Administration. Although many miles and
years would pass between each life-altering event, you would not
know it from our immediate and sustained gabfest when we reunited.
Then, as before, we would slip out of each other's lives once again to
await the next turning point.

Instead of my life always dominating our calendar, the next time
it was hers. Thelma thought the tummy pooch developing on her
tiny frame was just part of the typical aging process. Instead, it was
the growing deadly evil of stage-four ovarian cancer. Thelma is the
bravest person I know. I have known many brave souls in law enforcement who put their lives on the line every day, but they are trained
and prepared to do just that. As the head of the Drug Enforcement
Administration, I was credited with facing personal danger, but it was

Thelma who valiantly squared off against a very real Goliath time and again, beating it and gearing up to face the battle again all too soon.

Thelma is the kind of friend you hope to be—the one who remains strong for everyone else. When Thelma's oncologist—clearly a professional accustomed to disappointment—had to report yet another round of bad news to her, he didn't have to say a word. The tears in his eyes said it all. More concerned for him than for herself, Thelma started joking that she needed the doctor's closer parking space more than he did and announced her intention to re-label the doctor's reserved space in the dead of night with her own name.

I always admired those people who collect and connect friends and make the care and feeding of such friendships a priority notwithstanding everything else going on in their lives. I have racked up scores of well-intended but unfulfilled New Year's resolutions, vowing to be a better friend—to stay in touch, to remember birthdays and anniversaries. Instead, all too often, I moved on and either forgot or failed to take the time to look back, nurture, and hang onto the friends I left behind. Friends often become the first casualties for workaholics like me. When Thelma became sick, I vowed I would get it right this time. I would no longer live regretting calls I intended to make but didn't get around to or lamenting the time lost along the way as we lived our separate lives. No more lapses or gaps. What a blessing to have a second chance, when it mattered most.

On Christmas Day, we curled up on Thelma's bed recounting our funny high school memories. The next day, we were off to chemotherapy, with "frequent-flyer" Thelma upgraded to her requested "window seat." I cannot remember any subject too sensitive or off limits between us, including arrangements at the end of life. As usual, Thelma and I sat and laughed through that discussion as well. We went through the basics—whether it should be open casket (only if she looks good), and what clothes (her favorite teal blue, and no shoes!). She saved all the specifics for the party she wants us to have after the funeral and the practical jokes she wants me to execute for her after she is gone. Just in case God steps in to shake things up, I gave Thelma my own wish list—comfy clothes and no belts! We were meant to be.

Thelma thinks I am the successful one in life. I know it is she. She is my model—the pillar of strength, great courage, and grace. Just knowing her makes me a better person. I have had many friends throughout my life. Many were and still are close friends. But Thelma is special. We have a trust between us built block by block

through time and experience. My two daughters now know Thelma
and love her as I do. It is bizarre for someone who always fell short
of being perfect at friendship; mine with Thelma will be one of my
most important legacies. If my girls have learned anything from me,
one day they will find and treasure the crazy, adorable "Thelma" in
their lives.

---

*Karen Tandy is a Senior Vice President of Public Affairs and Communications for
Motorola, Inc., overseeing Motorola management in 72 countries. Prior to joining
Motorola in 2007, Ms. Tandy served as Administrator of the United States Drug
Enforcement Administration (DEA), where she managed approximately 11,000
employees across the United States and in 86 foreign offices. Before her service as DEA
Administrator, Ms. Tandy was Associate Deputy Attorney General, responsible for
developing national drug enforcement policy and strategies. Ms. Tandy previously held a
variety of positions in the Criminal Division of the Department of Justice and served as
an Assistant United States Attorney in the Eastern and Western Districts of Virginia.*

The Duty of Candor

Honorable Paul D. Clement

EVERY LAWYER HAS A DUTY of candor to the court as part of his or her obligations under the rules of professional conduct. Rule 3.3 of the Model Rules of Professional Conduct bears the title, "Candor toward the Tribunal," and outlines the lawyer's duties, inter alia, to avoid false statements of law or fact, to correct any inadvertent mistakes of law, and to disclose controlling adverse precedent. Georgia Rule 3.3 is to the same effect.

In the Office of the Solicitor General, candor to the Court is much more than an abstract principle or minimal duty of professional responsibility. It is the Office's modus operandi and a vital element of the Office's special relationship with the Supreme Court of the United States. The Office of the Solicitor General represents the United States government in the Supreme Court of the United States. And, of course, the United States government is far and away the most frequent litigant before the Supreme Court. For example, nearly half of all petitions for certiorari filed in the Supreme Court arise out of cases in which the United States prevailed in the court of appeals.

A number of practices of the Office of the Solicitor General are closely associated with the Office's tradition of erring on the side of candor in an effort always to maintain the Court's confidence in the accuracy and integrity of the Office's filings and representations. One clear example is the Office's long tradition of "confessing error" in cases in which the Solicitor General determines that a lower court's judgment in the government's favor cannot be defended in the Supreme Court.

In a typical year, the United States prevails in something on the order of 3,500 court of appeals cases in which the losing party files a petition for certiorari in the Supreme Court. In the overwhelming majority of those cases—close to 90 percent—the government waives its right to file a brief in opposition. In about 10 percent of the cases, the government prepares and files a brief in opposition. But on occasion, the Solicitor General does something almost no private lawyer would ever do. After reviewing a petition that argues that the court of appeals' opinion in the government's favor is wrong and inconsistent with the Court's precedent, the Solicitor General files a brief that explains that the petitioner—and not the lower court opinion in the government's favor—is correct.

Such a confession of error is not a step that any Solicitor General takes lightly. After all, the government will not ingratiate itself to many court of appeals judges if it makes a habit of telling the Supreme Court that the court of appeals' decision that the government just procured is not only wrong but well-nigh indefensible. But although a confession of error is not without its costs and not a step to be taken lightly, it is a step that virtually every Solicitor General has taken and it is a practice with deep roots in the traditions of the Office. It is also a practice that not only reflects, but reinforces, the Office's dedication to candor to the court. As one of my illustrious predecessors, Archibald Cox, explained, the Solicitor General's willingness to confess error "affects the way all our other cases are presented. If we are willing to take a somewhat disinterested and wholly candid position even when it means surrendering a victory, then all our other cases will be presented with a greater degree of restraint, a greater degree of candor, and with a longer view, perhaps, than otherwise."

Another slightly less dramatic practice of the Office that also reflects and reinforces the Office's dedication to candor to the court as a value is the practice of acquiescence in a petition for certiorari. A typical petition for certiorari argues not only that the decision below was wrong, but also suggests that the decision below contributes to a split of authority among federal courts of appeal or state courts of last resort, and that the underlying issue is important. A couple of times a year, the Solicitor General will file a brief that concedes that the petition is correct on two out of three propositions: the decision below contributes to a conflict in authority and addresses an important issue, and therefore, even though the government believes that the decision below was correct, the Court should take the case for plenary review. Such an acquiescence in certiorari is yet another prominent example of the Office's tendency to look beyond the government's narrow interests in the outcome of a particular case to the broader, long-term interests of the government. And in the long-term, no one case is more important than maintaining the Office's credibility with the Court.

While practices like confessing error and acquiescing in certiorari are dramatic examples of the Office's dedication to candor, that dedication is evident in the day-to-day work of the Office and in the arguments the government makes and refrains from making in all manner of briefs. As Solicitor General Cox observed, the confession of error is a manifestation of, not a deviation from, the Office's general approach to briefing and arguing cases before the Supreme Court. Two examples—one from before my time in the Office and one during my tenure as a deputy—illustrate the point.

The United States government often participates as an amicus curiae in criminal cases arising out of the state courts, and generally participates, if at all, on behalf of the State. That practice reflects the reality that many issues of constitutional criminal procedure equally affect state and federal prosecutors, and whatever the Supreme Court decides about the federal Constitution in a case arising in the state system is likely to affect federal prosecutors as well. In some cases, however, the State advocates a position that the federal government does not think it can fairly support. Such a situation arose in a case involving the requirement that officers knock and announce before entering a home. When the issue came before the Court in *Wilson v. Arkansas*, the State argued that the Fourth Amendment did not include any "knock and announce" requirement. Based on an exhaustive review of the common-law history, the lawyers in the Office of the Solicitor General determined that the State's broad no-knock rule was simply not tenable. Accordingly, the government filed a brief in support of the State, but one that eschewed the broad, no-knock rule for a more nuanced position that there was a common-law requirement that officers knock and announce, but the common-law rule was subject to exceptions, including exceptions that covered that particular case.

As it turned out, this was an example of the reality that candor with the court is not only a good practice, but is also good advocacy. When confronted with the numerous questions raised by the absolute no-knock position and asked what was wrong with the position of the Solicitor General, the lawyer for the State embraced the Solicitor General's position as a fall-back argument. At that point, Justice Antonin Scalia helpfully advised, "Time to fall back."

The United States also files briefs as amicus curiae in civil cases in which the government is not a party but an important government interest is nonetheless implicated by the case. When the government has satisfied itself that it has an interest in the outcome of a case, it, almost by definition, has an interest in the Court actually resolving the issue that prompted the government's participation in the case. But the government's interest in having the Court resolve an issue does not trump the government's broader interest in candor to the court. Accordingly, when in the course of preparing an amicus brief supporting a petitioner in a case involving the interaction of class-action rules and the amount-in-controversy requirement, the government recognized a problem with the lower court's jurisdiction, it did not hesitate to point out the issue to the Court even though the jurisdictional obstacle would prevent the Court from correcting a lower-court practice the government thought was erroneous. The government's brief included a long footnote, which explained that depending on the characterization of the District Court's order it was not an appealable order and appellate jurisdiction was lacking. As it turned out, that one footnote rendered the other 29 pages of the government's brief irrelevant. The Court ordered supplemental briefing on the jurisdictional question, and ultimately dismissed the petition as improvidently granted after an oral argument consumed by the jurisdictional issue. The Supreme Court has not had an occasion to revisit the issue since.

The candor shown by the Office in cases like these furthers a special relationship between the Supreme Court and the Office of the Solicitor General. That special relationship is manifested in a variety of ways. Perhaps the most concrete manifestation is the fact that the Solicitor General has a ceremonial office in the Supreme Court building, making the Solicitor General one of only two government officials with an office in two branches of the government (the other, more prominent example being the Vice President of the United States). Another manifestation is the Court's practice of inviting the Solicitor General to provide the views of the United States at the certiorari stage in cases in which the United States is not a party. The Court issues such invitations roughly 20 times a year, and they are the kind of invitation that no Solicitor General would dare refuse. But the very fact that the Court actively solicits the Office's view as to whether a decision was correctly decided, whether it implicates the interests of the federal government, and whether it satisfies the Court's criteria for plenary review is a manifestation not only of the special relationship but of the value of candor. Needless to say, if the Court loses confidence in the candor of the representations of the Solicitor General, such invitations will not be forthcoming.

The special relationship between the Supreme Court and the Solicitor General has caused some to refer to the Solicitor General as the "Tenth Justice." Whenever I mention that moniker, I am quick to add that I have never heard any of the nine real Justices use that term. Another of my illustrious predecessors, Drew Days, suggested that the "35th Law Clerk" more appropriately captures the relationship. But in many ways, the phrase that best captures the relationship is one that the Court itself does embrace in every volume of its official reporter, the United States Reports. At the beginning of each volume, immediately below the listing of the Justices, there is a listing of the Officers of the Court. Even before the more obvious candidates, such as the Clerk of Court, the Reporter of Decisions, the Marshal, and the Librarian, each volume lists the Attorney General and the Solicitor General. And, indeed, the candor that typifies the relationship between the Office and the Court is ultimately a reflection of the fact that every lawyer in the Office takes very seriously his or her role as an Officer of the Court.

Of course, the lawyers in the Office of the Solicitor General have no monopoly on the title Officer of the Court. Every lawyer is an Officer of the Court, and every lawyer would benefit from viewing that responsibility—and the duty of candor—as more than an abstraction, but as the way to practice law.

Paul Clement was the 43rd Solicitor General of the United States. Following graduation from Georgetown University and Harvard Law School, Mr. Clement clerked for Judge Laurence H. Silberman on the District of Columbia Circuit and Justice Antonin G. Scalia on the United States Supreme Court. Mr. Clement has argued 49 cases before the United States Supreme Court.

Yes Is Easy; No Is Important

Ron L. Olson

HAVING THE COURAGE to express your convictions in the face of an important client's proposal is a challenge most lawyers—young and old—periodically face. Affirming your client's proposal with enthusiasm is easy. We can all do that. But if you believe the proposal is outside the bounds of law or morality, can you muster the courage to say "no" convincingly? Saying "no" is a skill all of us must master. It will be among your most valuable services to your clients.

The first step in responding to a client's proposal is to fully understand the dimensions and implications of the proposal. Seldom are all of the nuances obvious to either the client or the lawyer at first glance. Deep thinking and careful probing are the necessary tools. A mistake I too often made in my early career was failing to question the client's position, thinking that doing so would reveal my lack of knowledge of the client's business or my inability to comprehend his or her seemingly obvious points. But the failure to probe at this early stage can lead to a faulty analysis premised on misunderstanding. Deeper questioning may also help the client recognize that the proposal failed his or her objective.

So step one in meeting this test is to understand the proposal clearly. Step two is to conduct the critical legal analysis fundamental to a lawyer rendering a judgment. Most law schools focus 90 percent of their teaching on legal analysis, and there's little I can add. Suffice it to say that the first answer to a difficult problem is usually not the only one, or the best one.

Clients have a right to expect your hard thinking about how their proposal can be justified within the law; however, a lawyer who's every response is "no" will soon be speaking only to himself. The tool that I find most useful at this stage is the mathematician's practice of inverting the proposal or the tentative conclusion. Write or think through the opposite proposal or conclusion to determine whether it is equally or perhaps even more convincing. If so, retreat to the library for more thought and critical analysis.

If after careful consideration your judgment is that the client's proposal is outside the bounds of the law or morality, or detrimental to your client's reputation or business interests, and mere adjustments to the proposal won't change the fundamental conclusion, then that judgment must be delivered—and delivered convincingly. Saying no with courage and conviction is a challenge. But if the plan is not appropriate or you cannot advise it, say so thoroughly and directly.

It is often said that the most valuable thing a lawyer sells is his judgment. I believe that to be true—but only when the judgment is accepted. The ability to gain agreement, in my opinion, makes the difference between a good lawyer and a great one. Acceptance depends on how thoughtful and objective your analysis is and how effectively you have communicated it to your client. Recently, an investment banker and I were engaging in the postmortem of a failed merger. We initially congratulated ourselves for having spotted the key issue and for reaching what later proved to be the right advice. But we quickly realized that being right was of little solace and reward when the merger had cratered precisely because our client rejected our advice. Good advice has little value if it is not communicated in such a way that it is followed.

My point is simple: Making the right judgment is important, but getting it implemented is more important. Here psychology may be as important as the law—the art of persuasion in and out of court is little understood and less appreciated in most law schools. However, it is a skill that lawyers must learn to master.

Nearly every important client proposal will sooner or later be exposed to others. One way to persuade a client to objectively examine a proposal is to subject it to what one client of mine calls the *New York Times* test. I remind my client that few important decisions are secret, and sooner or later, their decision will be exposed to scrutiny. My question to them is this: Would you be prepared to have your decision reported on the front page by an intelligent but unsympathetic reporter and read by your family and friends?

Another tool is to expand the discussion to include other people with different specialties and opinions. Test a proposal from a narrowly focused division manager with the company's CEO. If it is the CEO's proposal, run it by another lawyer or the company's board of directors. Get as many perspectives as you can to ensure that the proposal is solid and ultimately beneficial.

Vetting a proposal with others can expose flaws in the decision-making process and lead to a more comprehensive understanding of why and how a new idea can be advanced. Understanding and exposing irrationality in a proposed idea, or the methodology used to get to that idea, can sometimes be helpful in persuading a client to a more correct decision. Unfortunately, learning the psychology behind irrationality is not easily done; nor is learning how to counter that irrationality. My founding partner, Charles Munger, took it upon himself to do both and has set forth his learning in lectures published in *Poor Charlie's Almanack*.

As Munger illustrates, a good way to begin learning about flaws in decision-making can be chronicling and analyzing examples of bad judgment. You will be surprised by how many errors in judgment are explained by the same short list of psychologically based tendencies. The book *Influence* by Robert Cialdini will also give you a head start in identifying people's persistent thinking flaws. Once you understand these flaws, it can help make your analysis and conclusions more applicable and persuasive.

One of my main takeaways from Charles Munger and Robert Cialdini is that a key to business success is thinking through reasons before giving opinions and advice and, in doing so, giving your clients a full and thoughtful account on how you reached your decision. Your clients will be more likely to follow your advice if they understand and appreciate the reasons behind it. Good reasoning makes advice—even if it's not the answer they want—easier to believe in.

One notable practitioner of this was the famous engineer Carl Braun, whose highly successful company designed oil refineries with great precision and integrity. One of his simple but fiercely enforced rules for all managers was a requirement to specify with every order *who* was to do *what*, *where*, *when*, and *why*. An assignment that provided the first four answers but failed to include *why* was very likely to get the order-giving manager fired. Braun firmly believed that ideas (for me, in the case of legal advice, in the form of advice and opinions) are best understood and assimilated when the reasons for the ideas are detailed.

In sum, the lawyer's service to the client is, as most law schools emphasize, premised on a full understanding of the law, but it hardly begins or ends there. Asking tough questions about planned courses of action, and fleshing out all facts and nuances before you begin your legal analysis, will persuade your clients to accept and follow your judgments. It will also make you a more successful and valuable lawyer.

Ronald L. Olson is a partner in the Los Angeles office of Munger, Tolles & Olson LLP. He has served as a high-profile litigator and corporate counsel in a career spanning more than 40 years. In addition to a diverse law practice, Mr. Olson has served as a director at numerous companies including Berkshire Hathaway, and at nonprofits including the Mayo Clinic. Mr. Olson received his B.S. degree from Drake University in 1963, his J.D. degree from the University of Michigan in 1966, and a Diploma in Law from Oxford University, England, in 1967, at which time he was the recipient of a Ford Foundation fellowship. In 1967, Mr. Olson was an attorney for the Civil Rights Division of the Department of Justice and in 1968 clerked for Chief Judge David L. Bazelon, United States Court of Appeals for the D.C. Circuit. Mr. Olson is a fellow of the American College of Trial Lawyers.

Giving Back to Our Profession

Frank C. Jones

MANY YEARS AGO, I attended a dinner meeting of the Macon Bar Association honoring two members who had been appointed as judges. Even though there was already a full program, it was decided at the last minute that 10 Macon lawyers who had practiced more than 50 years should be invited to say a few words. All 10 accepted and, in most instances, the few words became a good many words, with the result that the program lasted until almost midnight.

I recall this event with pleasure. The 50-years-plus practitioners uniformly expressed pride in the legal profession and the satisfaction that they had experienced as lawyers. They evidenced their respect and affection for each other and for other members of the bar. They spoke with obvious conviction about the obligations of lawyers to the profession and to the public. The word "professionalism" was not then in vogue to the extent it is today but clearly they made reference to professionalism and its core values.

Many lawyers today are unhappy with their professional lives. A *New York Times* article concluded that, "Job dissatisfaction among lawyers is widespread, profound and growing worse." A bar publication reported that a survey revealed that more than 40 percent of the lawyers in a Midwestern state would not choose to be lawyers if they could make a career decision once again.

In her book, *The Majesty of the Law: Reflections of a Supreme Court Justice*, Justice Sandra Day O'Connor (Ret.) of the Supreme Court of the United States expressed the opinion that a decline in professionalism is partly responsible for this dissatisfaction. She quoted Dean

Roscoe Pound as saying that a profession is "a group . . . pursuing a learned art as a common calling in the spirit of public service—no less a public service because it may incidentally be a means of livelihood." She emphasized that following graduation from law school, lawyers assume the obligations of professionalism, which include obligations toward legal institutions and to the public. I agree fully with Justice O'Connor.

The Supreme Court of Georgia has adopted nonmandatory standards of professionalism that involve aspirations "higher than those required by the . . . rules of professional conduct. . . ." Many other appellate and trial courts have done the same. The Georgia Supreme Court urges that lawyers, judges, and legal educators adhere to certain "aspirational ideals," including the following:

(a) Improve the practice of law by participating in continuing legal education efforts, assisting in organized bar activities, and helping law schools in the education of our future lawyers;

(b) Provide pro bono representation that is necessary to make our system of justice available to all, and to support organizations that provide pro bono representation to indigent clients; and

(c) Strengthen our laws and system of justice by, for example, serving as a public official, assisting in the education of the public concerning our laws and legal system, and using other appropriate methods of effecting positive change in our laws and legal system.

Numerous other aspirational ideals applicable to lawyers' relations to clients, opposing parties, and their counsel, and to the courts and other tribunals, are also set forth.

All of these ideals are consistent with the concept of professionalism. Lawyers have a bountiful cafeteria of bar activities from which they may choose, either at the national, state or local levels. For example, the Directory of our State Bar lists 34 standing committees, 10 special committees, and 40 sections, and there are 26 Young Lawyers Division committees; no matter what one's practice may be, there is almost certainly a committee or section that should be of genuine interest to every lawyer and to which each of us can contribute. I believe that a lawyer who actively supports the organized bar and seeks to strengthen the profession itself, as distinguished from narrow practice concerns, almost always winds up being a better lawyer than otherwise would be the case.

Some years ago, Dr. James T. Laney, who was then the president of Emory University in Atlanta, spoke to a national professional group at my request. He selected the topic, "The Law—A Moral Aristocracy." He said:

> If I were to ask the numbers of [the group to which he spoke] who the most influential members of the bar have been in their lives, if you were honest you would probably not pick the ones who had the most lucrative careers, but the ones who had the greatest impact upon who you are and your values.

Every lawyer can make a real contribution to the profession by serving as a mentor for younger lawyers—by exhibiting as a lawyer the core values of professionalism. As the old saying goes, "I'd rather see a sermon than hear one any day."

I have now been practicing for more than 50 years. My feelings about the profession are the same as those expressed at the long ago dinner meeting in Macon to which I referred at the beginning of this essay. Notwithstanding our faults, I am proud of the legal profession. I believe there is a renewed interest in professionalism.

It is right for us to "give back" to the profession and the public by supporting the organized bar. We lawyers should give back some of our time and resources so as to benefit the profession and to better serve the public interest.

Frank C. Jones began his legal career more than 50 years ago in Macon, Georgia, at the firm now known as Jones, Cork & Miller, LLP. He later became a senior litigating partner at King & Spalding in Atlanta.

Mr. Jones has litigated a wide range of corporate and civil rights cases including arguments in the United States Supreme Court. Mr. Jones has served as President of the American College of Trial Lawyers, President of the United States Supreme Court Historical Society, President of the State Bar of Georgia, President of the Atlanta Symphony, and Trustee Emeritus of Emory University, and he serves on the Board of Directors of the Carter Center. Mr. Jones received his undergraduate degree from Emory University (B.A. 1947) and his law degree at Mercer University School of Law (L.L.B. 1950).

CHAPTER 17

Mentoring: Your Legacy to the Bar

John T. Marshall

IN NEARLY 50 YEARS of law practice, I have heard lawyers repeatedly espouse the value of mentoring to young lawyers. Moreover, lawyers and judges, without exception, recognize the importance of good mentoring in the development of competent, professional, and ethical young lawyers.

That lesson was brought home to me in my first year as a beginning lawyer, working as an associate in what was then a small firm. Here is what happened: After final arguments were over in a hard-fought trial, the judge had invited the lawyers to come to his chambers while the jury was out deliberating on a verdict. (The older lawyers and the judge were good friends, personally and professionally, over many years.) As we were all sitting in chairs grouped around the judge's desk, the talk turned to news of the bench and bar. One of the older lawyers remarked that old "So-and-So," a veteran trial lawyer at the Georgia Bar, had recently "gone to meet his Maker." To my surprise, the judge then asked, "What was it about old So-and-So that made dealing with him, in or out of court, so unpleasant?" After a moment of silence, the judge answered his own question. He said, "I think one of old So-and-So's main problems was that he simply wasn't 'raised right' as a young lawyer. Remember, he started out under [["another old So-and-So"]], carrying his briefcase. That was the only mentor he ever had. No wonder he turned out to be such a pain in the . . . !"

Just about that time, the judge was advised that the jury was ready to deliver its verdict. As the older lawyers were leaving the room, the judge reached for his robe and then motioned me to remain in his chambers. When the others had left, the judge finished fastening his robe and then turned to me and said, in a not unkindly voice, "Young man, you are fortunate to work at a good firm and to have a good mentor there. You will have no excuse if you turn out like old So-and-So! I hope you will remember that!"

Over the years, I have always remembered those words. And the judge was right. A young, inexperienced lawyer who has a good mentor has a gift that is priceless—to that young lawyer, as well as to our profession and its future.

In 2006, after 10 years of study that included a pilot project and a great deal of other work by numerous members of the Georgia Bench and Bar, the State Bar of Georgia recommended to the Supreme Court of Georgia that the state adopt a mandatory program to provide every beginning lawyer with a mentor for that young lawyer's first full year of law practice. The Supreme Court of Georgia authorized the mandatory mentoring program, which, at this writing, is completing its third year of operation.

Based on a number of reports from mentors and mentees in the program, I believe it is a success thus far. The mentoring program, however, has also had unanticipated, even surprising, effects on the lawyers who have agreed to serve as mentors for mentees inside or outside their firms. Let me give you some examples of what I am talking about.

First, the mentoring program has made many of the mentors remember goals they wanted to achieve when they entered the practice of law. Moreover, in many instances, mentoring has caused older lawyer mentors to renew their commitments to those goals.

For example, one mentor told me that he and his mentee had decided to take on a pro bono case as part of the program. As they worked on the case together, the mentor was reminded of his early years of practice where he occasionally represented clients who could not afford to pay. Today, and for a number of prior years, all of his clients were "paying clients." ("With," he added, "varying degrees of enthusiasm on their part!") He also recalled his law school years, during which he had vowed to himself he would always represent "at least some" poor people. As part of our program, he and his mentee tried a jury case together and obtained a small but "very satisfying" verdict for a pro bono client who had been wrongfully dispossessed.

After the "formal" mentorship was over at the end of the beginning lawyer's first year of practice, the mentor recalled again the goals of his law school years and early years of law practice, and decided to take on another pro bono project, this time with another young lawyer who had been employed at his firm for about two years. "Before long," he told me, "I found myself acting toward each of the two young lawyers just like the mentor that I never had the good luck to have in my beginning years."

A second example: The program has caused a substantial number of mentors to find that mentoring has enriched and revitalized their professional careers. A mentor told me that he decided to take his mentee to a regularly scheduled luncheon of his local bar association. As he introduced his young lawyer around, the mentor went out of his way to greet a number of lawyers that he had not run into for several months or even years. The mentor continued, "Since then, my young lawyer and I have gone to just about every regularly scheduled bar lunch. As I introduced my young lawyer to other lawyers at those lunches, I was reminded of how much I missed meeting regularly with my colleagues at the bar." He added, "Why, I might even run for President of that crowd, down the road."

A third example: The mentoring program has caused some mentors to examine more deeply traditional ideas about our profession that they had heard repeated many times and had pretty much taken for granted.

One mentor explained his experience like this: He and his young lawyer were driving back to their office after the young lawyer had just been sworn in by the local Superior Court judge who then charged all the young lawyers in the courtroom about the duties and responsibilities of their profession, much as she would charge a jury. The judge had started her charge by reminding the assembled lawyers, "We are members of a noble profession." As they rode along together, the young lawyer, remembering what the judge had said about a "noble profession," asked his mentor an unexpected question: "Although it's easy to say that we are a noble profession, have you ever seen opposing counsel act nobly in a hard-fought jury case?" The old lawyer thought about this for a few moments and then replied: "Yes, I have. It happened like this. I was defending a jury case many years ago where my clients were a father and his son who were charged together with negligence in causing the plaintiff serious personal injuries arising out of an automobile accident. Under the undisputed facts, where the son was driving, there was no question that the father, if liable to the plaintiff under the Georgia Family Purpose Doctrine, would be 'held' in the verdict."

During the course of pre-trial depositions, plaintiff's counsel asked the defendant father (in the presence of his defendant son) if the father had ever been convicted of a felony. The father answered, "No."

"In a break before the son's deposition began, the father pulled me aside and whispered, 'I lied in there during my deposition. When I was 21, I was convicted of armed robbery of a liquor store where the only thing I did was to drive the getaway car. I swore that if I ever got out of jail, I was going to be a changed man. And since then, I have been. I joined a church where I met the woman who is now my wife and our son's mother. I got a steady job. I have been a model husband and father. I have always trained my son 'to tell the truth, to obey the law, and do right.' But, I never told either of them or anyone else about that robbery and the time I spent in jail. If that comes out, and my family finds out that I am a felon and a liar, everything I have tried to be as a model for my wife and our son will crumble. Their lives and my life will be ruined.'"

The older lawyer continued, "When I told my client that he had to go back in there and correct his testimony 'on the record,' he refused. Knowing full well that the rules of ethics required that the lie not be allowed to stand 'on the record,' I went to opposing counsel and explained the situation. Since the father's liability under the Family Purpose Doctrine was unquestioned, I asked opposing counsel if he could 'see his way clear' to keeping my client's secret and to let me correct the father's testimony at a later time, without embarrassing the father in the presence of his son. Counsel's reply, 'Let me think about it.'"

"We then went on with the son's deposition. When the deposition had concluded and everyone was preparing to leave, my opposing counsel called me aside and said simply, 'You may tell your client that his secret is safe with me.'"

The older lawyer concluded, "You know, I have never really thought about that in this light, but I believe my opposing counsel's action in keeping my client's secret, under those circumstances, was a noble act, in the middle of a hard-fought case."[1]

When we began planning the mentoring program so many years ago, we had no idea how much the program would enrich, and sometimes revitalize, the professional lives of the experienced lawyers who served as mentors. In light of these and other experiences with the

---

[1] By the way, we settled the case some time later for reasons that had nothing to do with the father's perjured testimony.

mentoring program, perhaps it should come as no surprise that we have more experienced lawyers volunteering to serve as mentors than we have first-year lawyers who are mentees.

My hope is that those who are beginning lawyers today will go on to become the mentors of tomorrow. My expectation is that these mentors will shape the profession in years to come.

I do not believe it misses the mark to say that each generation of lawyers must learn lessons like these, and similar lessons, if our noble profession is to continue to be worthy of that description. The standards of our profession require that all of us bear a personal responsibility in seeing that these standards are not lowered. A vital part of this responsibility is that each of us must be willing to serve as a mentor to see that young lawyers are "raised right." The mentoring program is a strong, first step in that direction.

But, every lawyer's duty to mentor young or less-experienced lawyers does not stop in a program that only reaches younger lawyers in their first year of practice. Young or less-experienced lawyers need mentoring in their second, third, and fourth years of practice, as well as thereafter.

Each generation of lawyers in our profession must see that the standards of our profession are understood, maintained, and passed on to young or less-experienced lawyers who follow us. Otherwise, our calling will no longer be a profession. It will be "just a job."

In its own unique way, mentoring is a legacy that each of us owes to our profession and to those who follow us in the practice of law. But, like other legacies, to be effective, it must be bestowed.

Is there a young or less-experienced lawyer in your firm or locality who needs a mentor? If so, the legacy of mentoring that lawyer is yours to bestow upon that young or less-experienced lawyer, as well as upon our profession. The need for action is now, and not some well-intentioned later date. The only question is, "Will you act now?" Both that lawyer and our noble profession are waiting.

John T. Marshall is a senior litigator at Bryan Cave. Prior to the merger of Bryan Cave and Powell Goldstein in 2009, Mr. Marshall was a partner for over 40 years at the law firm of Powell Goldstein LLP where he chaired the Litigation Department.

Mr. Marshall is a former President of the Atlanta Bar Association and a former adjunct professor at the Georgia State University College of Law and Emory University Law School. Mr. Marshall is a Fellow of the American College of Trial Lawyers, a Member of the American Academy of Appellate Lawyers, the Panel of Mediators and Arbitrators of the American Arbitration Association, a Fellow of the Georgia Bar Foundation, and a Trustee of the Eleventh Circuit Historical Society. He presently serves on the Supreme Court of Georgia's Board to Determine Fitness of Bar Applicants and for a number of years has chaired the State Bar of Georgia's Committee on Standards of the Profession.

Mr. Marshall graduated from Vanderbilt University in 1956. After graduation from Vanderbilt, he served as an officer in the U.S. Marine Corps. He received an LL.B. from Yale University in 1962.

Legal Education and Formation
for the Profession of Law

Walter F. Pratt Jr.[1]

LAW SCHOOLS ARE IMAGED as *the* entry point into the practice of law. That image is often accompanied by an implication of responsibility— responsibility for both the knowledge and the conduct of those who practice law. Those of us who teach in law schools tend more readily to accept the former responsibility (for knowledge) than the latter (for conduct), especially since most questions about conduct arise only *after* conduct is deemed to be inappropriate. Rather than attempt to sort out the credit-blame pairing, I prefer to replace the term "law school" with "legal education." To me, the former presumes discontinuous, separate points—law school as separate from practice. By contrast, the latter sees the years devoted to earning a first degree in law as part of a professional life—legal education as an integral component of practice; and, for that matter, undergraduate education and much of life in general. In my preferred view, everyone is involved in legal education. Those of us who teach in what are denominated "schools" are involved in a particularly intense way, for our interval

---

[1] My thoughts about the role of legal education in forming professionals have been significantly influenced by two decades on the faculty at Notre Dame Law School. More recently two books have justifiably provoked widespread discussion, which has also had an impact on the ideas presented in this essay: The Carnegie Foundation's report, *Educating Lawyers: Preparation for the Profession of Law* (San Francisco: Jossey-Bass, 2007) [[the individual authors are William M. Sullivan, Anne Colby, Judith Welch Wegner, Lloyd Bond, and Lee S. Shulman]] and the volume by my colleague Roy Stuckey, *Best Practices for Legal Education: A Vision and a Road Map* (Clinical Legal Education Association, 2007).

is one in which we deal with novices, those who have only recently acted upon a belief that they are fit to become professionals. But it is critical to recognize that these novices come to "school" with already established images of what it means to be a professional. It is therefore essential that all in the profession—teachers, practitioners, everyone—recognize the importance of those pre-school exposures to the profession. Some exposure will have been through real-life practitioners; some will have been through fictional representations. Because those formative images are difficult to alter, it is essential that everyone in the profession recognize the impact of their conduct on this formative period. All professionals should acknowledge a duty to discuss these modes—real and fictional, good and bad—precisely because of their formative effect.

Those of us who teach in schools recognize that each novice brings a different mix of exposures. We therefore have a rich collection of experiences to help foster discussion. But we may also have a diverse set of expectations, making it difficult even to achieve consensus about what is appropriate conduct.

Of course, we can, and should, discuss the consensus that appears as the current iteration of rules or standards for ethical conduct. They inevitably provide a base for discussion. And, exposure to the rules can reinforce the novices' awareness of the import of choosing to become professionals, especially when the exposure begins on the first day of "law school." Use of the rules alone, however, is not sufficient to emphasize the distinctiveness of being a professional. It is both fortunate and unfortunate that we no longer have a distinctive garb, such a monk's cowl, that visually sets us apart from the world. Unfortunate in that there is no mark to emphasize this distinctive stage in the life of a professional. Fortunate, in that we do not too much emphasize the "apart." For, unlike monks, lawyers must live *in* the society of which they are a part. Indeed, lawyers are special precisely because they are called to be of service. In a society that exalts the importance of individual decisions—the market economy is the paradigm—the core of what it means to be a professional is to act in service to others, not in self-regarding interest. Our challenge, in dealing with the particularly intense educative phase of professional life is to ensure that the "other" is a part of all that we do. Thus, while a current version of rules may substitute for the cowl, its very distinctiveness threatens to isolate novices from those they are called to serve. That threat is made all the more potent by the many self-regarding influences that are a part of "school." Our challenge is to re-enforce the profession as dominated by the other-regarded, nonmarket interests rather than by the self-regarding, market interests.

The depth of self-regarding conduct's influence on law school is evident from the beginning, with the selection of a new class of novices each year. That process is dominated by grades and LSAT scores. To be sure, Peace Corps or AmeriCorps volunteers receive credit. But without a credible, single number, admission to a "top" law school is unlikely even for them. In short, from the start, the self-reflective numbers of grade point average and standardized test scores are crucial. Similarly, the standard teaching method in law school excludes any "other." Familiarly termed "Socratic," this method involves a professor calling on a single student to discuss some aspect of an appellate opinion. The singular focus emphasizes the one person; more importantly, the appellate opinion offers little sense of those actually involved in a dispute, the "other" to whom service as a professional should be dedicated. We continue the emphasis on self, excluding any "other," through our grading process, most of which is based on a single examination at the end of a semester-length course.

At the extreme, this emphasis on self can tempt to destructive conduct, with novices failing to share their learning (class notes) with others and even hiding or mutilating necessary research materials. More subtle is financing, with more and more novices depending on loans to pay for law school. The insidious nature of financing becomes apparent as soon as the discussion turns to some notion of "leveraging" one's future on the faith of being able to earn sufficient income in the future to repay with interest. Once that turn in discussion is taken, we have irretrievably moved to the notion of law as a business, in which income is essential to provide a return on investment. That focus inevitably is self-directed, to the exclusion of any other.

With so many parts of law school pressing toward the self, how might we modify legal education?

The core of my suggestions relates to my preference for "legal education" as a continuum, for at the core is a belief that the formation of novices requires the involvement of practitioners as well as those of us housed in the academy. We are all part of a community of learners. Our success in encouraging professional values depends upon our working together in common with one another.

To begin with admissions: Fairness requires that there be notice that something other than the self-directed numerical scores will play a key role. Indeed, that notice is one of the key elements to being a professional—the transparent act of revealing standards in advance, as

well as the ability to explain those standards. Letters of recommendation and lists of activities will play a key role. But, in the end, only
interviews allow the selection of those already inclined to be other-
directed. For those interviews, practitioners must be involved. Their
involvement can only be with a rigor that avoids personal bias, for
that is itself a form of self-direction. Instead, the interviews must be
conducted with the highest standards of concern for the well-being
of the profession.

Once admitted, novices must be shown the respect due any other
member of the profession. Just as providing notice of standards for
admissions is a way of modeling appropriate behavior, so must be
the conduct of professors in the classroom. The Socratic method has
merit insofar as it offers training in the skills likely to be needed as
practitioners; but implementation of the method should be done only
with respect for the novice, in ways that encourage further explora-
tion of skills and knowledge. Equally important, conduct of the classroom must encourage respectful dealing with those who disagree.
Beyond the method involved, the content of the courses, especially
those of the first year, should include the "other." Instead of relying
exclusively on appellate decisions, the class could watch video-clips
in which actors portray the parties. Here again, practitioners could
be involved to interview these actor-parties. Similarly, practitioners
could meet with small groups of students to critique both the interviews and the substance of the case.

Classes can therefore both teach substantive areas of law and dem-
onstrate appropriate "professional" conduct. A more difficult challenge arises when the topic turns to the formal rules of conduct—legal
ethics. The difficulty arises because of the near complete exclusion of
the "other"—discussions of rules without the potential for impact on
an actual person tends to be sterile. One response is to attempt to
integrate ethics into all courses—sometimes termed the "pervasive"
method. But that method, too, lacks personality.

A different method, almost an aside, is to teach through an honor
code or code of conduct. Every law school has a code of that sort.
But it is particularly important that the code be *taught* (as opposed to
waiting for a violation to occur before discussion). The importance
of teaching arises for at least two reasons. The first is related to the
influence of pre-school events. Increasingly it seems that few students arrive at law school with an understanding of concepts such as
plagiarism. For there to be an expectation that students will adhere
to a set of rules, there must first be an explanation of the rules. The

second reason is that for any profession to exist, its members must be willing to police themselves. Few, if any, novices understand the critical distinction between "ratting" on someone and enforcing professional obligations. Those in the academy can explain plagiarism and other concepts. But for an understanding of professional expectations, we should rely on help from practitioners. The ideal would be to have discussions led by those who have run afoul of ethical standards, teaching from their own example, possibly as a version of community service. More likely would be the use of practitioners to present the facts of real cases as part of a discussion with small groups of students. That model would work best if the practitioners could be senior members of the profession seconded to law schools for a period of time, as "practitioners in residence."

There is irony in my call for greater dialogue between the Bar and the Academy, as a continuum in legal education: If my call is answered, then we may risk encouraging the impression that new lawyers cannot find their way to the courthouse. For our portion of legal education would concentrate on enhancing the already extant sense that lawyers serve their communities, because that is the essence of formation. Nevertheless, I am convinced that the road to the courthouse will be much easier to navigate when illuminated by the wisdom of the profession.

Walter F. "Jack" Pratt Jr. is the Dean at the University of South Carolina School of Law, a post he assumed after serving on the faculty of The Law School, University of Notre Dame. He received his B.A. in History, magna cum laude, from Vanderbilt University in 1968, where he was a member of Phi Beta Kappa. He earned his D.Phil. in Politics from Oxford University, which he attended as a Rhodes Scholar. He earned his J.D. degree in 1977 from Yale Law School, where he served as the article and book review editor for the Yale Law Journal. *He was a law clerk for Judge Charles Clark, United States Court of Appeals for the Fifth Circuit (1977–78) and for Chief Justice Warren E. Burger, Supreme Court of the United States (1978–79).*

CHAPTER 19

Professional Courage

Larry D. Thompson

A WHILE AGO, I was preparing a speech dealing with, among other topics, the role of lawyers who represent public companies in the post Sarbannes-Oxley world. I wanted to point out that lawyers needed professional courage to properly and effectively represent public companies. As I reflected on the topic, I was immediately reminded of a memorable moment in my practice experience involving Judge Griffin B. Bell. When I spoke, here is how I told other lawyers about the need for courage and principles in the practice of law, and how I was taught that important value by Judge Bell.

Regarding the corporate scandals of 2002, as Linda Thomsen, head of the SEC's Enforcement Division, has noted, "[m]uch of the conduct [of lawyers surrounding the 2002 spate of corporate scandals] was not actionable; but it wasn't admirable either."

The corporate scandals of 2002 were devastating. Billions of investor dollars were lost—almost overnight. Confidence in our financial markets was completely shaken. The blunt question asked by Judge Stanley Sporkin in connection with the savings-and-loan scandals of the 1980s is still relevant, "Where were the lawyers?"

So, on this point let me turn to the Report of the Task Force on the Lawyer's Role in Corporate Governance issued in November 2006 by the New York City Bar Association. The Report cites the work of Neal Batson of Alston & Bird in the Enron bankruptcy proceedings. Neal found with respect to Enron that we lawyers did a number of things. We correctly identified problematic conduct by company officers, we indicated our concerns about potential unlawful conduct, but we then did not follow through with forthright advice to the Board or other senior lawyers. For whatever reasons, some economic, some associated with professional pressures, lawyers wavered or equivocated when faced with giving unwelcome advice to powerful corporate officers.

So what does the Report recommend? Well, the Report's central recommendation is remarkably brief. In fact, it's just two words: "professional courage." For the Report's drafters, professional courage is the "indispensable element" needed for us lawyers to avoid the problems leading up to the scandals that occurred in several large public companies.

All of this reminds me of a time in the mid-1980s after I returned to King & Spalding as a partner. Judge Bell had just established the white-collar and government investigations practice he called special matters. We were ready for business, especially the myriad investigations into procurement fraud aimed at almost every large and mid-sized defense contractor. Well, we soon got a call to represent a large defense contractor located outside of Atlanta. Judge Bell and I flew to meet the General Counsel and other prominent lawyers from around the country the company had already retained. In the ensuing discussion about the case that followed, Judge Bell and I became very concerned about how things were being discussed. Judge Bell mentioned his concerns to the General Counsel, but the same discussions continued. I then looked over and saw Judge Bell putting his papers in his briefcase and then saying to me, "Come on, Larry, we need to go." The General Counsel was shocked but was eventually able to persuade Judge Bell to stay. However, the uncomfortable and inappropriate discussion ceased.

That, to me, was a vivid and living example, early in my career, of professional courage—the ability to walk away from questionable conduct and, if necessary, to exercise the obligation to fire a client who insists on engaging in conduct that a lawyer's good conscience, judgment, and integrity cannot condone.

Larry D. Thompson is PepsiCo's Senior Vice President, Government Affairs, General Counsel and Secretary. Prior to joining PepsiCo, Mr. Thompson served as a Senior Fellow with the Brookings Institution in Washington, D.C., and taught as a visiting professor at the University of Georgia School of Law. From May 2001 to August 2003 he served as Deputy Attorney General of the United States under President George W. Bush, which included leading the National Security Coordination Council and President Bush's Corporate Fraud Task Force. Earlier in his career, Mr. Thompson served as the United States Attorney for the Northern District of Georgia before entering private practice. Mr. Thompson graduated with a B.A. degree from Culver-Stockton College, has an M.A. degree from Michigan State University, and earned his law degree from the University of Michigan.

Epilogue

WHETHER WE INTEND TO OR NOT, each of us influences the conduct and lives of those with whom we work, especially younger coworkers in whom we have taken a special interest. This is particularly true in the interaction of lawyers. It is no surprise therefore that two of our essayists here independently recount the same formative incident, from their different perspectives, without seeing each other's essay. Thus, Judge Bell recalls the occasion when a client suggested an inappropriate course of action, and he instructed the young associate accompanying him to pack up because they were leaving. That young associate was Larry Thompson. That incident had a profound impact on Larry as well, and he recites the same story from his own perspective in his essay here. Larry also often recounts this same incident in speeches he makes about his life as a lawyer. He simply is passing along to other lawyers what Judge Bell passed along to him—an unshakeable and fearless commitment to integrity. Passing along the lessons we have learned from those who have gone before us is part of our obligation to our profession. It is our privilege to pass along the lessons and guidance reflected in these essays, and we hope you might return to them from time to time, knowing you are among old friends who share this journey with you.

The Editors